THE
ELECTION MEN

THE
ELECTION MEN

Professional Campaign Managers
and American Democracy

David Lee Rosenbloom

 **Quadrangle Books**
A New York Times Company

Library of Congress Card Number: 72-91380
ISBN 0-8129-0308-0

For my parents

Soap and education are not as sudden as a massacre
but they are more deadly in the long run.
—MARK TWAIN

Acknowledgments

The idea for this book was born in the fall of 1968 when Jack Saloma, then of the MIT political science department, recommended that I examine the growth of the professional campaign management industry in my Ph.D. thesis. A brief mention here seems to be an inadequate way to thank my advisor and friend, but I shall always be grateful to Jack for the time, energy and talent he invested in me and my work. Ithiel Pool, then chairman of the MIT political science department, was also continually available for help and advice, for which I am thankful. I also want to thank John Steinbruner of Harvard, John McCarthy of Yale, Dan Rich of the University of Delaware and John Blydenburgh of the Eagleton Institute of Politics at Rutgers for making valuable suggestions at different stages of this effort. Thanks too go to Harold Faber for his substantial editorial assistance.

Graduate school is a bargain only if you do not have to pay for it yourself. In my case, the Woodrow Wilson Foundation paid for a year of my preparation and for most of the research that went into the thesis upon which this book is based. The MIT political science department also contributed a grant that covered the costs of computer analysis of most of my information. Through a Ford Foundation grant, Hamilton College made it possible for me to take the time needed to update and rewrite the thesis. I am grateful for this support.

The professional campaign managers of the country were extraordinarily generous with their time. Most of them submitted to interviews that lasted from 1 to 4 hours; almost all of them filled out and returned a complicated questionnaire that took at least an hour to complete. I believe that many managers will agree with my conclusions, even though they are critical. They know what they are doing; if the rest of us do not react, it is our tough luck. Other managers will take strong exception to my interpretation of their intentions and work, and I look forward to a continuing dialogue with them.

One of the problems I discuss in the book is the accountability of managers for their work in American elections. Therefore, I want to make my own position clear. I share responsibility with all those mentioned above and with many more who have been helpful for what is correct about this book and I accept responsibility myself for the errors in judgment that undoubtedly will be found.

D.L.R.

Clinton, New York
June, 1972

Contents

ix

CHAPTER 1

The New Gang in Town

> We have created a Government by grin. Elections in America have become a big, profit-making business, with professional campaign management firms at the center of virtually every major election campaign.
> —*A consensus of the managers.*

American elections have changed in recent years. The politicians who run in them, the journalists who cover them and the people who vote in them all agree that something strange has been happening. Edmund S. Muskie, the Democratic front-runner in the 1972 Presidential campaign, drops out of the primaries. John V. Lindsay turns his back on the Republican Party, becomes a Democrat, runs for the Democratic Presidential nomination and then withdraws for lack of support. George S. McGovern, who does poorly in the public opinion polls, surprises many by his strong showing in the primaries. Hubert H. Humphrey resurrects himself from the politically dead and emerges once more as a Democratic contender. On the eve of the Presidential election of 1972, President Nixon flies off to Peking and then Moscow.

The voters are understandably uneasy. Their actions at the polls in the 1972 Presidential primaries demonstrated a discontent with things as they are, a malaise that seemed to be growing. In the late 1960's, polls showed that political parties were our least respected political institution and that the vast majority of voters thought that too much money was being spent on politics, especially on television advertising. The polls also showed an increasing level of cynicism and pessimism about politics among the public in the late 1960's and early 1970's.

Analysts and pundits who looked at the results of the past

1

few elections have found contradictory information, predicting almost anything their hearts and political predilections desired. Kevin P. Phillips, the apostle of the new Republican majority, found the voters on the right. Richard M. Scammon and Ben J. Wattenberg predicted that the real majority would be in the center. Fred Dutton, a Kennedy New Frontiersman from California, saw the future in the young people. And Walter DeVries, an academic cum campaign advisor, found the influential voters to be moderate, independent-minded ticket-splitters. These and other tea leaf readers have tried to envision an incipient or actual realignment of political forces in each confusing electoral result; if a realignment actually does take place, at least one of the analysts will look brilliant because every possible rearrangement of the electorate has been predicted by someone.

But perhaps the emphasis on voting studies and statistical analysis has caused us to look at the wrong place to understand what has been going on in our electoral system. The ferment that is being reported in the electorate may be more apparent than real. The fundamental changes, in fact, may not be related to ideological shifts by the voters at all. They are probably remaining relatively steady, trying to find their own interests and voting them. That may be increasingly difficult if everything else is changing.

A look at recent elections shows that it is the election process itself that has undergone the most basic change. Campaigns are now ridiculously long and phenomenally more expensive, waged principally through commercial media like television and radio, through direct mail advertising and on the telephone.

Campaigning for public office has now become almost a continuous process, with planning for individual campaigns spanning virtually the entire period between elections. McGovern formally announced his candidacy for the Democratic nomination more than 18 months before the actual election and by the Spring of 1971 he had a professional staff of more than 40. Muskie did not bother to announce his candidacy until the beginning of 1972, but even before his candidacy collapsed, he had gone through at least four turn-overs in professional campaign staff leadership. By the late fall of 1971, the Committee to Re-elect the President had organized, collected many millions of dollars, tested campaign themes, and selected key precincts for polling and test marketing of commercials and campaign issues.

Elections in America have become a big, profit-making business, with professional campaign management firms at the center of virtually every major election campaign. In fact, political campaigning is one of the biggest growth industries in the country.

Exact figures on the growth of the campaign business are hard to come by but even the rough estimates that are available show that the amount of money spent in political campaigning has been doubling every four years recently. About $100 million to $150 million was spent in pursuit of the Presidency in 1968, and more than $200 million was probably spent in the 1972 campaign. Up to $1 billion may have been spent in pursuit of all the elective offices available in the United States in 1972.

The single largest expenditure by candidates is for television and radio, and some accurate figures are available to show the sharply rising costs. In 1960, candidates for public office spent $14,195,000 for broadcast time; by 1968 the figure had risen to $40,403,000. In 1970, an off-Presidential year, candidates invested $50,292,164 in television and radio time. And these figures include only the amounts paid for time on radio and television; they do not include production costs, which have been rising rapidly, too. For example, one top level producer charged a candidate about $30,000 in the early 1960's to produce a half-hour campaign documentary; in 1970, the same type of production cost $90,000.

Congress has now acted to cut the growth in spending on television campaigning. A new law limits the amount of money candidates can spend on television and radio to not more than six cents a constitutent, and forces stations to charge candidates the lowest rates. However, money not spent on television will be spent elsewhere. As one example, computer-written direct mail appeals, which are not covered by the new law, were one of the fastest areas of growth in the 1970 campaign and continued to grow in 1972. At a cost of between ten cents and 15 cents a letter, computerized direct mail can eat up money faster than it can be minted.

With the growth of new techniques in the use of television, polling and computers, a new set of political managers has emerged at the center of American elections to direct their use. Professional campaign managers are the new gang in town. In the broadest sense, a professional campaign management firm is a company that provides services for pay to candidates for public office, to political parties and to groups supporting or opposing public referendums. The services these firms offer range from full responsibility for planning and executing an entire campaign, including recruiting and training the candidate, to very specialized detailed services like polling or graphics design.

There are about 300 firms in the United States that provide any or all of these services, including many advertising and public relations agencies that handle limited portions of campaigns. There are about 100 firms in the country that regularly manage political campaigns in the sense that they accept principal responsibility for planning and executing all aspects of a campaign. In the past few years, agents of these firms have been centrally involved in most of the major election campaigns in the country.

There is nothing really new about the existence of paid political advisors and it should not come as a shock to anyone that candidates for public office have advisors. Most of us first learned about them when as children we were told the story about the emperor and his new clothes. The people who introduced the "magic" tailors to the emperor, who first admired their work and advised him to show his new "clothes" to the masses, were political advisors.

What distinguishes the new crew of professional managers from those in the past is not their increasing sophistication alone. The traditional political advisor was dependent on his relationship with one politician or one political group, like a local party committee, with his fate depending on the fate of the politician for whom he worked. The modern professional campaign manager seeks to break that dependence by establishing a base of his own, a private, profit-making company; he is a businessman as well as a politician. He looks at elections and sees a billion dollar market. As one of them said, "This is a business and I'm interested only in the candidates who will spend."

Professional campaign managers are in the center of the great expansion in campaign spending. The growth of their industry is both a cause and an effect of the rise in spending. Professional campaign managers recommend to candidates techniques that cost lots of money. Candidates see other politicians spending vast sums and feel they must do the same if they are to survive.

Since professional campaign managers are in business to win campaigns and make money, it is logical to assume that they recommend techniques that will make them the most money. And they do. The evidence of their operations in campaigns bears this out; if a choice has to be made between a less expensive and a more expensive course of action, professional campaign managers very often choose the more expensive way.

From its inception, the professional campaign management industry has been associated with the growth in the use of commercial and commissionable advertising in political campaigns. The first professional firm, Whitaker and Baxter of California, was both a professional campaign consulting firm and an advertising agency. Many of the latter-day firms have tried to match this lucrative combination.

The rise of professional campaign management in American elections deserves the closest study because the changes it reflects and brings go to the very heart of our political system. The legitimacy of our politics is wrapped in the cloth of elections. To tear at this cloth is to tear at the heart of democracy itself.

Elections are the core of democracy for a very simple reason. If we believe that "all men are created equal," counting their preferences at election time is about the only way we can make decisions and have them accepted. When all are equal, there is no real reason for one to defer to the other. Of course, we have never fully implemented this simple belief. The most favorable assessment of our political history suggests that we have moved haltingly and erratically in the direction of achieving our revolutionary assumption of the basic equality of humans.

Both the quantity and quality of participation are essential elements of a democratic political system. Counting the people's choices on Election Day is central, but so is the quality of the process that precedes Election Day. Any election can choose leaders by counting, but not all elections would be judged equally democratic. For those who believe in democracy, an election is a great opportunity for the citizen to engage himself in his own future. The election process must allow the citizen to determine his own interest and vote it, thus contributing to his own self-development and expression.

Elections in a democracy produce two things, governors and legitimacy. The winners of elections get not only power but a general acceptance of their right to wield it. Any election can give the winner power. Only a democratic election can give the winner both power and legitimacy. For example, for most of the century that followed the Civil War, elections in the South conferred power on a small white elite, but the great bulk of these elections were not in any sense legitimate since blacks and many poor whites were prevented from voting. Minor disputes among the ruling elite were settled in closed primaries, and general elections were often uncontested. The people who ran the South got power through sham elections and kept it by economic and physical repression against people who might otherwise oppose them. Federal intervention aimed at improving the quality of electoral participation perhaps has begun to change that. The closed primary, poll taxes, many discriminatory registration practices and literacy tests have all been outlawed in the South over the last 25 years. Some of the tools of economic repression have also been attacked by the spreading industrialization of the South, by Federal intervention and by outward migration of some of the most oppressed people. The extraordinary political and economic repression that marked the political atmosphere of the South in the past is almost all gone, but even in 1970 there were 42 completely uncontested House elections in the 11 states of the Confederacy, of a total of 49 in the entire country.

The cumulative effect of the electoral system in the South has had a direct bearing on the collapse of the legitimacy of the Congress as the nation's principal representative lawmaking body. In the past 30 years, we have seen a tremendous shift of power from the Congress to the Presidency, caused at least in part by a growing belief that the Congress was unable or unwilling to respond to modern problems. The Southern-Democratic conservative coalition that has controlled the Congress for most of the last 30 years is the product of uncontested and undemocratic elections. Perhaps that is one reason we have looked to the President and the bureaucracy to respond to our national problems.

A similar case can be argued for the lack of faith many Americans express toward their state legislatures. For most of the 20th century, rural areas retained control over state legislatures because they refused to reapportion themselves to account for the shift of population to the cities and suburbs. Until the one-man, one-vote rulings of the Supreme Court in the 1960's, the patently undemocratic state legislatures got the public support they deserved—very little. People knew that the electoral system that produced their state legislatures was a sham so they gave it very little attention. Throughout the century, fewer than half the eligible people have participated in state legislative elections. Now that state legislatures have been reorganized to reflect the population realities of their states, more people may begin to think of them as legitimate institutions worthy of their support and attention.

Federal intervention in the electoral system of the South, court-ordered reapportionment of the state legislatures, the 18-year-old vote amendment and the Democratic Party rules reforms are all part of a historic process toward greater democracy and more genuine mass participation in politics. With the major exception of voter registration reform, the United States has moved a long way toward creating a legal framework for full and genuine political participation for all people.

However, the connection between the nature of the electoral system and the legitimacy of the results should make us look at the professional campaign managers very carefully. While recent legal actions may have been designed to expand both the quantity and quality of electoral participation, the emergence of professional campaign managers and the changes they are bringing to politics may well offset these gains. The commercialization of American politics may deny us the kind of participant democracy that has finally been coming within reach.

Professional campaign managers have a singular view of the electoral process. They get paid to win; they do not get paid to worry about either the quantity or quality of voter participation. The techniques they use are supposed to help their clients win. That is all. Their goal is votes, and that is not necessarily the same as democratic participation in decision making. As businessmen, professional campaign managers are more interested in the profitability of elections than in their quality. In this sense, the professional campaign manager is concerned solely with the part of elections that helps choose leaders. The part of the election process that grants legitimacy to the victor is not really his problem. His contract ends on Election Day.

While we have been busy refining our laws to open political participation to all of our citizens, professional campaign managers have been busy making our elections commercial advertising ventures. While we have been guaranteeing access to the ballot for all our citizens, professional campaign managers and the techniques of commercialized politics have been closing access to candidacy to all but the rich and the photogenic. If the 1970 elections are indicative, we are in trouble. The professional managers and their techniques dominated those elections—on both sides. Obviously many of them lost major races. When two professional managers are facing each other, one will lose, even though both rely on the same commercial techniques and artificial organization.

We have gone well beyond the problem of one candidate sweeping through to victory with professional techniques. Now, all the candidates are using the professionals and their techniques, and it is the consequences of this new kind of politics that we must examine. We should remember from our frontier days that things did not "even out." When both the ranchers and farmers hired their own gunmen, the countryside got bloodier. Professional managers on both sides of a campaign do not restore a balance—they create a new kind of war.

CHAPTER 2
The Emergence of the Professionals

Ottinger delivers.
> —*Richard L. Ottinger, Democratic candidate for the U.S. Senate from New York, 1970.*

Burton,A Man to Match the Mountains.
> —*Lawrence J. Burton, Republican candidate for the U.S. Senate from Utah, 1970.*

The President asked me, "What do you need?" I told him I needed a professional campaign manager, a professional media manager and substantial financing from outside the state. . . . They were delivered.
> —*Thomas S. Kleppe, Republican candidate for the U.S. Senate from North Dakota, 1970.*

The professional campaign managers came into their own during the 1970 Congressional elections. At times it seemed that the commercial rivalry between campaign managers overshadowed the candidates and the elections themselves. *Time, Newsweek* and the press covered the campaign managers almost as much as the actual contests, a clear sign that professional campaign management had become an integral part of election campaigning. By 1970, it was obvious that professional campaign managers had arrived at the focal point of political campaigns as the alternative to local and state political parties.

The flowering of professional campaign management on a national scale had its roots in the 1950's when mass-merchandising techniques were first used in a modern way to sell political candidates. In 1952, for example, the Republicans made effective use of advertising and public relations techniques in Eisenhower's first campaign for the Presidency. In his study of that campaign, Stanley Kelley, Jr., of Princeton University said:

> The strategy, treatment of issues, use of media, budgeting, and pacing of the Eisenhower campaign showed the pervasive influence of professional propagandists. The Democrats used fewer professionals, were less apt to draw upon commercial and industrial public relations experience in their thinking, and their publicity men apparently had less of a voice in the policy decisions of the campaign.

By 1956, as television began to grow into its role as the predominant vehicle of mass communications, the men who knew how to use television, the TV advisers and even the make-up men, increased in importance. Image began to replace reality not only on the screen, but in the thinking of the men behind the candidates. Even in Congressional races, commercial selling practices were seen as guides for politics and elections. Leonard Hall, chairman of the Republican National Committee, predicted that the Republican Party would carry Congress that year because "it has a great product to sell. . . . You sell your candidates and your programs the way a business sells its products."

As the new powerful tools of mass manipulation became more available to politicians and candidates, a new breed of managers arose, men who were familiar with the intricacies of managing public relations, advertising, polls, computers and television—the professional campaign managers. Their growth during the 1960's was phenomenal. In 1960, there were probably fewer than 25 professionally-managed races for the House of Representatives; but in 1968, these had risen to at least 125.

Just as the Republicans led the way in the use of the new tools in the Presidential campaigns, they also used them more frequently in the lesser races. In the period 1960 to 1970, for example, the Republicans relied on professional managers for Congressional races twice as frequently as the Democrats. One of the reasons was that the Democrats had dominated the Congress for almost 40 years, with members of long standing building up powerful permanent campaign organizations as part of their own staffs. Especially in the House of Representatives, Democrats did not feel the need for specialized intelligence research prior to an election because staff members conducted soundings throughout the period in office.

On the other hand, Republicans have had to make up for their organizational weakness in their attempt to gain control of the House and Senate by relying heavily on professional campaign management firms to gather information about Democratic districts, to recruit candidates and to run the campaigns. In 1966, for example, the Republican Congressional Campaign Committee and the Republican Booster Committee commissioned polls in more than a hundred Congressional districts. In some of these, they hired firms to search for good candidates; in a few, they sent the firms in with enough dollars to do the job.

The Republicans staked their hopes for winning the 1970 Senatorial elections on attractive candidates and professional campaign managers. The President personally recruited many of the Republican Senatorial challengers and he and his aides then sent them the professional help and money they needed. Professional campaign managers were dispatched from the White House, the Republican National Committee and the Republican Campaign Committees to plan and run campaigns all over the country.

The experience of Thomas S. Kleppe, the Republican candidate for the Senate from North Dakota, was typical. He told a reporter: "The President asked me, 'What do you need?' I told him I needed a professional campaign manager, a professional media manager and substantial financing from outside the state. These things were deliverable, and they were delivered."

His Democratic opponent, Quentin N. Burdick, the incumbent, also brought in professionals and received bushels of outside money. Both sides polled and advertised extensively, spending about three times as much money on the campaign as they had six years earlier. Kleppe lost, receiving only slightly more than one-third the vote, but the new professionals, one behind each candidate, couldn't lose.

The President's own media manager in 1968, Harry Treleaven, went to several of the target states, including Tennessee, where he and William E. Brock III, the conservative Republican challenger, faced off against Albert Gore, the liberal Democratic incumbent, helped at the last minute by Charles Guggenheim, another professional media man and film maker.

The successful Brock campaign in Tennessee was a model of the new professional politics. In April, 1969, more than 18 months before the election, Ken Rietz, a 27-year-old associate of Treleaven, arrived in Tennessee for the first time. He wandered around the state for a couple of weeks, did some preliminary research and then wrote a campaign strategy for Brock's 1970 campaign. The plan programmed the activities of the candidate from June, 1969, through Election Day, 1970. Brock agreed to follow the plan, to pay Rietz close to $40,000 for managing the campaign and to pay Treleaven to create the media advertising effort. Before they were through, Rietz and Treleaven spent more than a million dollars. They built a statewide organization independent of any other political body and produced a media campaign blitz that was unlike anything ever before seen in Tennessee.

For one of the ads, Treleaven took over a football stadium, brought in 250 supporters, jammed them into a small place to create the appearance of a crowd and made a film of an enthusiastic Brock rally, with crowds cheering on cue. That phony ad was a perfect summation of modern election campaigning. Rallies, whether in village squares or on railroad sidings, had been a central element in campaign communications, a way for the candidate to rouse the voters and campaign workers. In modern politics, rallies are merely a device to get the candidate good television coverage. At virtually all political rallies today, the candidate is not talking to the people in front of him, but to the people he hopes will see him on television. The message he is delivering is not in words, it is in pictures of a crowd cheering. Treleaven knew that before most politicians. He created his own rally for the television cameras he controlled and showed it to the people on time he bought.

Gore, the Democratic incumbent, did not know how to react to this onslaught of the new politics. In the past, Gore had been successful by campaigning in the old-fashioned way, by returning to Tennessee from Washington, traveling around the state and talking to individual voters or small groups. The serious threat being mounted by the well-planned and expertly-executed Brock campaign was perceived by Gore's aides much more quickly than he saw it. But it wasn't until August, just three months before the election, that the Gore campaign became organized in a modern sense. Guggenheim was hired to help with television advertising, with substantial amounts of money flowing in from labor unions and peace groups to help him get his product on the air.

Guggenheim came in from Washington and followed Gore around the state for days, filming him playing checkers with an old friend, riding a white horse, talking to workers and businessmen. From 16,000 feet of film, Guggenheim created a dozen 30- and 60-second spot commercials to play against Brock's. The whole campaign, near the end, took on the look of an old-fashioned range war, with the hired guns fighting it out for the sheepmen and ranchers.

It would be too simple to say that Brock won solely because Treleaven produced better commercials than Guggenheim. Tennessee was a state in political transition, moving toward the Republicans. Nixon had carried the state in 1968 with 38 percent of the vote, trailed by Wallace with 34 percent, and Humphrey behind them with 28 percent. More than that, Brock had an attractive running-mate for governor, Dr. Winfield Scott, who had spent years building the Republican organization in Memphis, while Gore was running with the controversial John Jay Hooker, who was having well-publicized financial troubles with several of his corporate ventures. In addition, Nixon had made Gore the number one target of the 1970 campaign, and the Republicans poured money and manpower into Tennessee to defeat him.

What Rietz and Treleaven did was to put it all together in a winning combination. Their carefully-planned, well-executed campaign over a period of more than a year prevailed over Gore's long years of service and his last-minute attempt to match their television blitz.

Treleaven and Guggenheim also squared off against each other in Michigan. Treleaven attempted to change the image of a complete newcomer to electoral politics, Lenore Romney, the Republican candidate, while Guggenheim worked for Philip A. Hart, the Democratic incumbent. Mrs. Romney had helped her husband, George, in his campaigning for governor of Michigan, but in 1970 she was on her own—except for Treleaven's direct communications creations.

He was paid $20,000 for a biographic film that showed Mrs. Romney to be the nice person that she was, and $200,000 more was spent to put it on television. Her name recognition went up, but the polling showed that her support did not. The voters regarded her as a nice but non-political person. To try to change that image to one of a tough, fighting candidate, her managers ordered a series of commercials attacking Hart. The new Romney ads said things like, "Good grief, haven't we had enough Hart trouble?" It didn't work. The hard-line ads were dropped when public reaction showed that they were confusing, and Mrs. Romney returned to being a nice person in the ads as well as privately.

Mrs. Romney lost the election, by a two-to-one majority, once again showing that professional campaign managing is not always successful. In a campaign in which two professional managers are on opposite sides of the election, one of them obviously must lose the election; but both of them win when candidates spend hundreds of thousands of dollars for the services they sell. They win by changing the ways in which campaigns are conducted toward their image of a campaign.

What happened in Tennessee and Michigan was repeated all over the country, and, in addition to one professional campaign manager winning and one losing, there was one big loser in each of the campaigns—the local party. Professional campaign managers took control of both sides of major campaigns and focused their research, planning and advertising directly on the voters, ignoring for the most part the state and local political parties. The extent to which local parties were ignored became clear after the election. In Utah, the Republican state chairman, Fred T. Wright, and two colleagues wrote a letter to Washington that summed up the resentment of the local leaders.

They charged that an Administration-recommended campaign management firm had come into the state and caused the loss of several important elections, including the Senate race. The firm had run a hard-line media campaign, matching the Republican, Lawrence Burton, with the mountains and trying to couple the Democrat with violence and crime. In some ads, Burton rode onto the screen on a horse, got off and attacked the Democratic incumbent, Frank Moss, for being in favor of crime, war and violence. The state leaders complained that there was no coordination between the campaign management firm and the party, arguing that "if there had been a coordinated effort these seats could have been won." They warned that the firm would never be allowed back into the state to work on a Republican campaign.

Whether or not the state leaders in Utah will be successful in throwing professionally-managed politics out of the state is far from clear. The clearer message from the 1970 elections is that candidates and their financial backers have now found an effective way to do without state and local political parties.

While Republicans took the initiative in general elections with professionals, some Democrats turned professionals on other Democrats in primaries, adding a new dimension and price tag to Democratic family squabbles. In the New York Democratic Senate primary in 1970, David Garth delivered the nomination for Richard L. Ottinger, an attractive and wealthy Congressman who wanted to be Senator. Like many members of Congress, Ottinger was virtually unknown outside his district. The professional planners decided that the way to win the Democratic primary was to make Ottinger's name a household word. They created a series of ads that corresponded to the theme, "Ottinger Delivers." They pictured the candidate as a tough and aggressive go-getter on issues like the environment, which he was, and spent almost two million dollars to show the ads on television. By the time the primary campaign was over, Ottinger was a household name; he won the primary, upsetting the candidate of the regulars, Theodore C. Sorensen, the former John F. Kennedy aide, and two other liberal contenders, Paul O'Dwyer, the left-liberal New York labor lawyer, and Representative Richard McCarthy of Buffalo.

But primaries are different from general elections and the New York election in November, 1970, was a maze of Byzantine maneuvers. The incumbent, Republican Senator Charles E. Goodell, who had been appointed to the seat of the assassinated Robert F. Kennedy by Governor Rockefeller, was jammed down the throats of unwilling Republicans by Rockefeller, himself a candidate for re-election. Goodell had alienated a large section of his party by his transformation in the Senate from a typical conservative upstate party man into a liberal, anti-Vietnam war activist. Even though his over-all party record indicated more general support for President Nixon than opposition, his criticism of the Vietnam war brought Vice President Agnew into the state, campaigning against him and for the Conservative Party candidate, James L. Buckley.

The Buckley campaign was managed by F. Clifton White, the conservative who had master-minded Barry Goldwater's nomination in 1964. White's first problem was to get the Buckley name recognized. A name recognition poll in March, 1970, showed that despite Buckley's race for the Senate two years before when he collected a million votes, only 17 percent of the voters in New York could identify him. Ordinarily that would be fatal. But White went beyond mere name recognition. He looked at the ideological distribution of the New York electorate and found that about two-thirds of the voters considered themselves moderates or conservatives. He thought this was a large enough pool of potential supporters, since his candidate would need only about 38 percent to win in a three-man race. The results proved White correct; Buckley won with 37 percent of the vote.

Ottinger, who was the front-runner early in the campaign as a liberal Democrat in a state that traditionally votes for liberals, was trapped by liberal support of Goodell. Nixon's opposition to Goodell had created a small swell of support for him from liberals in New York, who thought the enemy of their enemy must be their friend. It was clear that Goodell could not win; it was equally clear that Buckley was gaining. Ottinger's problem was to maintain his own base of support by preventing defections on both the right and left.

The three-man race made hash out of Garth's campaign, which had been so successful in the four-man primary. The Ottinger campaign seemed to run out of steam. Ottinger, who had spent a fortune in the primary, ran out of ready money as the general election neared and he was forced to cut back on his television campaign. In his personal appearances, he also seemed to lose some of the drive that had characterized him as a Congressman.

During the primary, Garth had managed to keep almost complete control over the flow of messages and information from the candidate to the people. Even Ottinger's appearances on regular news shows blended with his commercial image because he used the same stage setting for news announcements and press conferences as he did for his advertisements. One image—an active doer—was consistently transmitted; it is almost a trademark in Garth-run campaigns.

That image was Garth's campaign, when it was under his complete control. In the primaries, all the voters knew about Ottinger was what they had seen on television commercials; few people had ever seen him in person. Ottinger is a likable, thoughtful, shy man who got results as a Congressman by hard work, long hours, a large paid staff and a responsiveness to the needs of his district, all of them worthwhile qualities. But in large groups, in debate and on panel shows, he came across as stiff, a plodder, anything but the vital doer of his television ads. In the closing days of the campaign, the contradiction between the candidate and his image was too glaring.

Bearing in mind the complexities of the three-man race in New York, it would be too much to say that Ottinger could have won if his managers had been able to hide him, relying on television commercials alone, but many professional campaign managers do precisely that by discouraging press conferences, uncontrolled live appearances and debates. Garth's campaign for Ottinger is cited by him as an example of why professional campaign managers should rely almost completely on formal media they can control.

In the mid-1960's Joseph Napolitan's firm had full management responsibility for Milton J. Shapp's primary and general election campaigns for governor of Pennsylvania. According to Napolitan, he participated in or made almost all of the key strategy decisions in the first Shapp campaign. The first, and key decision, was that Shapp should run.

A name recognition poll told Shapp that he was not identified by large numbers of Pennsylvania voters, but neither were most of the other potential candidates. Napolitan's advice was, "Run." His rationale was that Shapp could buy statewide name recognition faster and more effectively than the other candidates. Shapp had the money and Napolitan knew how to buy name recognition with commercial advertising.

Napolitan supervised the attempt to get Shapp the endorsement of the Pennsylvania Democratic Policy Committee and when that failed, he planned the campaign strategy of running Shapp against the Pennsylvania Democratic machine. The theme, "Man against the machine," was the focus of all the primary advertising, which included a thirty minute biographical film shown frequently on television. Shapp won the primary.

In the general election, Napolitan used techniques similar to those in the primary, though Shapp made an abortive attempt to take over the machinery of the state Democratic organization by pushing his own man for chairman. Not having control of the party apparatus, Napolitan used a strategy that relied heavily on direct mass communication with the voters. The campaign prepared and mailed a 16-page booklet about Shapp and his program to every Pennsylvania household, and carried on a radio and television saturation campaign in the closing weeks of the election.

Napolitan did his last full poll for the campaign in October, 1966. It showed Shafer (the Republican) "ahead and likely to win." Napolitan recalled that as a pollster he would have had to conclude that Shafer would probably win, but as a campaign manager he had confidence (misplaced as it turned out) in his ability to swing that massive undecided vote to Shapp in the final ten days of the campaign.

Shapp lost the election. Napolitan attributed the loss in part to the general dissatisfaction with the national Administration and the conditions in the cities that were expressed in the Republican trend throughout the country and in part to a low voter turnout in Democratic areas. Since Democrats had not been asked to participate in the campaign until Election Day, it is not surprising that many of them stayed home.

The Napolitan effort for Shapp showed how professional managers could take a person with no experience in politics and unknown to the public and the party cadre and make him a major candidate for public office. By the end of the campaign, Shapp's name recognition in the state was higher than the Republican candidate's even though Shafer had been lieutenant governor for four years. Shapp truly ran for governor on his own, even paying for most of the contest himself. All the people were asked to do was vote. About 250,000 fewer Pennsylvanians went to the polls to vote for governor in 1966 than in 1962. Most of the voters who stayed home were registered Democrats and Shapp lost by less than 200,000 votes. By the time he ran for governor in 1970, Shapp had learned enough about politics to rely on local talent and use more than the mass media. He won.

Ronald Reagan was another 1966 candidate who knew nothing about politics. He hired a hot-shot California firm, Spencer-Roberts, to run his campaign. Under the firm's direction, Reagan was introduced to Republican leaders all over the state and speaking engagements were arranged both in and out of California. They hired another firm, Behavior Science Company, to supply substance for his speeches in the form of small note cards and briefing books on every conceivable topic. After its initial soundings, Spencer-Roberts decided Reagan could be elected if he were not too closely identified with Goldwater. Using their experience as directors of the 1964 Rockefeller California primary, they recruited moderate Republicans to serve as local chairmen of the Reagan for Governor campaign.

The firm reported that it had a major role in identifying and turning out the Reagan vote in the Republican primary, but the regular party organization assumed that burden during the general election. In both instances, door-to-door canvassing was done to determine a voter's preference. If the voter was for Reagan, the campaign organization made special efforts on Election Day to make sure he voted. The firm shared responsibility for the advertising program with the agency hired for the campaign, McCann-Erickson, whose California office was headed by Reagan's brother. Spencer-Roberts was responsible for the general design of the advertising approach, and McCann-Erickson produced and placed the advertising.

The management firm also had responsibility for organizing the citizen support groups in the campaign and for scheduling the candidate. It reported that the controlling factor in establishing the candidate schedule was "whether the occasion would present a good opportunity for television news coverage."

Reagan knew nothing about politics, but Spencer-Roberts did. They made a virtue out of Reagan's ignorance. They called him a "citizen-politician" who should not be expected to know all the answers, and hit the theme so well and hard that by the end of the campaign Governor Edmund "Pat" Brown was on the defensive for being a "professional politician."

Reagan won the election by a million votes and Spencer-Roberts got both cash and credit. Strong Reaganites say he would have won if Mickey Mouse ran his campaign, but prior to his race for governor, Reagan had no experience in politics; Spencer-Roberts did.

Almost immediately after his stunning election victory, Reagan was talked about as a possible conservative Republican candidate for President in 1968. Nothing was done to squelch the talk, and planning for an assault on the Republican convention began. White, architect of the Goldwater drive in 1964, was retained to teach Reagan all about Presidential politics. Once again, Reagan was moved around the country to meet the party politicians and faithful, and he quickly became the hottest item on the Republican fund-raising circuit. Throughout 1967, he made speeches, met Republican leaders and helped raise millions of dollars for Republican coffers.

For the 1964 campaign, White had decided to wage a fight

through the primaries to get Goldwater known around the country and to get grassroots conservative Republicans into positions of power in the party. The strategy for Reagan in 1968 was precisely the reverse. His past fame as an actor and on the fund-raising circuit was enough to get him known. Besides, Reagan probably could not beat Nixon in many primaries. In 1968, White would play a waiting game.

An unwitting partnership with Rockefeller could deny Nixon a first ballot majority at the convention; then Reagan would appear from the right-wing to save the party. White knew all the Republican leaders around the country; he knew that many of them were going with Nixon only because they thought he was a winner. Ideologically and viscerally, they wanted Reagan. White knew that there was enormous latent support for Reagan among the Southern delegations to the convention. All he needed was to get enough of them to withhold first ballot support for Nixon; this, combined with Rockefeller's votes, could possibly stop Nixon.

Just before the convention opened, Reagan announced that he was available for the Presidency, an announcement that had not been planned. White had hoped to hold off for a while and not alert the Nixon forces that he was eating away their Southern strength. Once Reagan announced, however, the formal battle was on. The Nixon forces fought desperately to hold on to their Southern strength.

An excellent convention operative, White came close to success. He succeeded in getting many contingent promises for support; that is, a bloc of Reagan supporters within a state promised to vote for Reagan if another group would. Many delegates promised support on a second ballot. Some of the politicians who were there insist that the Reagan forces were within five votes of putting the whole puzzle together. The keystone was in the Florida delegation, where Reagan had about a dozen delegates who were openly prepared to support him on the first ballot. He had another bloc within the delegation that was prepared to do the same thing, if he could get a few others who were wavering. If the White organizers had gotten these few people, they would have had a majority of the Florida delegation on the first ballot. That was supposed to set off a chain of vote switches that would have stopped a first ballot victory for Nixon.

It was all very "iffy," but that is not the point. Reagan, the would-be President, did not have to know anything about Presidential politics. He had hired an expert to teach him what he needed to learn and to organize the whole thing. In one move, Reagan and his friends bought all the political expertise about Republican Presidential politics that Nixon had spent his life learning.

When it was all over, Reagan went back to California to be governor again. Spencer-Roberts was retained to plan and run the 1970 re-election campaign almost two years before the actual election. Reagan had learned a lot about politics, but he thought they still knew more, a belief that was not shared by some members of his staff. They thought that one term in the state capitol had taught them enough to plan and organize a campaign on their own. As a result, Spencer-Roberts did not have as free a hand in 1970 as it did in 1966.

Throughout the campaign there were continuing disagreements with the governor's staff about strategy and tactics. The firm's polls showed that Reagan was collapsing toward the end; in October, Reagan dropped almost 17 percentage points in the polls. As a result, his campaign strategy shifted. Originally, his managers had assumed he would have time to campaign for members of the state legislature as well as for himself. But when his own support started to fall, he resumed campaigning for himself, and managed to win, with a 500,000-vote margin over Jesse Unruh, the Democratic candidate.

After the election, many politicians and observers were critical of the Spencer-Roberts effort, even though it did not have a free hand. Reagan's margin of victory, the politicians said, was about half the size of his 1966 margin even though he spent more than two-and-a-half times as much money as Unruh. The Spencer-Roberts image was tarnished, but its campaigns for Reagan, like White's campaign for Buckley and Napolitan's for Shapp, showed what professional management could do with newcomers to politics.

The professional campaign managers have provided an opportunity for special interest groups and rich individuals who feel that the nation needs their leadership. They have become the teachers and organizers for a whole new breed of politician; they have made it possible for men and women who have been successful in one field to go directly to the top of another without starting at the bottom again. It is no longer considered necessary to know something about politics to run for public office. The monopoly of knowledge held by party leaders and elected officials has now been effectively broken by professional campaign managers.

CHAPTER 3

The Tools of the Trade

> Parents who have little girls who are Brownies are precisely the kind of people who will vote for our Republican candidates.
>
> *—Vincent Barabba, campaign researcher.*

> When you want to pick cherries, you go where the cherries is.
>
> *—Matt Reese, campaign manager.*

The Hubert Humphrey who ran for the Democratic nomination for President in 1972 was just as much a re-made man as Richard Nixon was in 1968. His producers tried him out in Minnesota in 1970, a remarkable demonstration of how completely professional managers and media men have taken over American electoral politics. There in full color on television, a candidate for the U.S. Senate, was the new Humphrey, his hair a little thicker and blacker than it used to be.

Humphrey in 1970 was managed and produced by Sherman, Valentine and Associates of Minneapolis, Jack Chestnut and their computers. Gone were the old friends and staff from 20 years of fighting for liberal causes. The new breed of managers put together a new Humphrey, all on television, all based on computer analysis. Not even his announcement for the Senate was made in person; he taped it the day before and then released it for distribution. During the campaign, Humphrey was on television frequently, always under completely-controlled circumstances. His managers were quite proud that their candidate went through the entire campaign without holding any press conferences at all.

The heart of the new Humphrey was a computer. By Election Day in Minnesota, the campaign managers had built a data bank that included essential information on more than 80 percent of the Minnesota voters, who they were, where they lived, their phone numbers, party, past voting experience, their current preference in the campaign and lots of other things. Using this information, the computer "wrote" hundreds of thousands of "personal" letters to Democratic leaders and voters all over the state, helped plan the areas Humphrey and his media campaign should emphasize and told campaign workers which voters should receive telephone calls on Election Day.

The major difference between the Humphrey campaign and the other 1970 elections was that he did not ignore the Democratic Party and the other Democrats running in his state; he took them over. The Humphrey organization ran the whole show, and the payoff was handsome. Humphrey won, as expected, and the Democrats regained control of the state house. But it was a private Humphrey organization that did it, not the party.

The Minnesota victory was essential for Humphrey's still-active Presidential ambitions. When he went back on the Presidential trail in Florida in 1972, Sherman, Valentine and Jack Chestnut—and their computer—were there with him. The Humphrey campaign was not run on issues, but on time—a major change on both counts. Some of his television advisers were back from the 1968 campaign, but this time they had plenty of opportunity to create a proper advertising approach. Humphrey came in second in that primary, but his chances for the Democratic nomination improved tremendously. He went on to win in Ohio and Indiana.

Humphrey had learned a lot from his defeat in 1968, when to the very end, he insisted on remaining a real, live candidate. In 1968, he made as many public appearances as he could and held press conferences as often as possible. He almost missed the beginning of his final nation-wide television appearance because he wanted to speak to just one more group of the faithful at a union hall. He always looked tired and rushed on television, not a confident image of a powerful Presidential candidate.

Just as Humphrey's Senatorial campaign in 1970 was a prime example of the new politics, his 1968 campaign for the Presidency was the last gasp of the old politics. Following the chaos of the Chicago convention, Humphrey stumbled on toward Election Day, with little money, little help and a divided party. He recovered, he reorganized, he finally got the professional help he needed, but down to the end, his campaign was a mixture of the old and the new.

When Joseph Napolitan arrived at the offices of the Democratic National Committee in Washington in September, 1968, to take charge of the media campaign, he felt like running down the hall, shouting, "The election is November eighth, the election is November eighth." He had been convinced by the lack of planning that nobody there knew when Election Day was, a violation of the first law of professional campaign managers: that everything in a political campaign is planned to come together on Election Day, the last day on their flow charts and advertising schedules.

Napolitan and his crew of film makers, television producers, advertising men and pollsters went to work. They were not much different from the men who "sold" Richard Nixon but they were smart enough to throw Joe McGinness out so he could not write about them. Of course, they had more problems than the Republican campaign managers. Rent by the real problems that divided the country—the war, violence, race—the Democratic Party was a mess because its leaders and followers were divided on those very real issues.

Humphrey started the campaign with lots of press conferences and public appearances because that was the only way he could get on television. He had no money to buy time and no fancy ads to show. People came to shout at Humphrey at meetings because he was a relevant symbol of disastrous public policies. He was real.

The Republican managers had it much easier. Their campaign ran like clockwork. The balloons went up on time. The audiences were polite and controlled and their candidate always looked scrubbed and "new." Nixon dealt with the war by implying that he had a plan to end it, and he handled most other issues by saying it was time for a change. All was calm and peaceful, the way the Republicans planned it. Nixon was ahead and no one wanted to rock the boat. All he needed to do was keep Republican voters happy and pick up some of the Democratic defectors. The Republican managers planned a non-campaign to avoid provoking anybody to vote against the resurrected Nixon. They conducted a campaign that was totally irrelevant to what was going on in the country. Kids did not shout at Nixon the way they did at Humphrey because he did not relate to anything that concerned them. Reporters did not rattle Nixon at press conferences because he did not have them. Communication with the press was by handout. Nixon did not need the press because he could get his message directly to the people in his own words on commercial radio and television time. Everything in the Nixon campaign was controlled.

The professionals brought into the Humphrey campaign scrambled to bring it under similar control. To the professional managers, control meant getting a single theme for the campaign and their decision was that Humphrey and Muskie were to be symbols that the voters could trust. With six million begged and borrowed dollars, the message went out in 30- and 60-second spots that the Humphrey campaign was on the march. Humphrey put the Vietnam issue to rest in his Salt Lake City speech on September 30th, which was, in effect, a declaration of independence from President Johnson. Shortly after that, his ads started appearing on television and the viewers saw Humphrey in peaceful confident settings.

In the strange world of commercial politics the campaign got going when the controlled ads got on the air.

The commercial resurrection of Hubert Humphrey succeeded in 1970 and it showed signs of success in 1972. What happened in the Humphrey campaign and in other campaigns around the nation in 1970 highlighted the role of the professional campaign manager and his tools—the computers, research, the polls and television.

Professionally-managed campaigns are different from traditional campaigns because the managers have a different view of the election process and because they do different things. For the traditional party politician and candidate, the election is part and parcel of their continuing contact with the electorate, in which they receive a feedback from the public from their visible reactions during a campaign. Each election comes in the context of all the elections that preceded it and the necessity of governing after the election. The sole concern of the professional manager is the election at hand. For the professional manager, each election is a problem that can be solved by adequate research, planning and management. Neither the past nor the future is relevant.

As a result, professionally-managed campaigns look alike, taking essentially the same form. They begin with detailed demographic and survey research that leads to formal planning. The plans are then carefully and expensively executed. Professionally-managed campaigns are almost always self-contained, wholly under the control of the campaign manager. Commercial advertising, usually on television, direct mail and telephone banks are among the forms most frequently employed by the professionals to communicate with the voters.

Even the professionals who rely on door-to-door campaigning create for each campaign instant organizations that disappear after Election Day. Some statewide campaigns have mobilized as many as 10,000 volunteers to call on their neighbors, but when the campaign was over, they disappeared back into their homes and offices without leaving a trace.

The core of professionally-managed campaigns is research. Most professional managers simply refuse to become involved in a campaign unless the candidate agrees to at least a minimal research effort. There are four different kinds of research that professional management firms supply to campaigns: demographic and past voting behavior studies, opinion polling, issue research, and research about the opposition and they often begin 18 months before an election.

Public opinion and voter behavior research is a new way of doing a traditional political task: collecting current and accurate intelligence about the electorate. Keeping track of the opinions and predicting what the voters would do has always been a principal task of precinct level party workers. George Washington Plunkitt of Tammany Hall described what he did to stay in touch:

> To learn real human nature you have to go among the people, see them and be seen. I know every man, woman, and child in the fifteenth district, except them that's been born this summer—and I know some of them too. I know what they like and what they don't like, what they are strong at and what they are weak in, and I reach them by approachin' at the right side.

Abraham Lincoln gave campaign advice to the Whigs in Illinois that is still used by some Republican firms as a guide to their activities:

> Divide the county into small districts and appoint in each a committee . . . make a perfect list of the voters and ascertain with certainty for whom they will vote . . . Keep a constant watch on the doubtful voters and have them talked to by those in whom they have the most confidence. On Election Day see that every Whig is brought to the polls.

Traditional political organizations relied on personal contact between a party worker and the voters for continuing political intelligence and guidance for campaign planning and policy actions. The precursor to demographic research was that party leaders knew where voters were and how they behaved.

The traditional approach has been replaced for several reasons. First, the organization was never as pervasive and accurate as its memorial myth makes it; there was a lot the old-timers did not know.

Second, the personal communication base of the traditional political intelligence system is considerably more difficult to maintain in a society which has doubled its population since Plunkitt was alive and is considerably more mobile. The population base of a voting district now changes substantially every year. A telephone list that is six months old is often 35 percent wrong. However, population growth alone is not a satisfactory reason for the decline of personal intelligence systems. In fact, Plunkitt's district was more densely populated and voter turnout was higher when he was district leader than it is today.

Third, formalized research is expensive, but it is cheaper for a candidate or party hierarchy than the traditional personal system. Some of the resources the traditional party organization had are just not available today, especially government jobs for the regular party workers. These resources have been replaced by cash to pay for accurate political intelligence about a district.

Finally, the information gathered through formal research is available to anyone who can pay for it, whereas the information of a traditional political organization is available only to its leaders. Moreover, the formal techniques allow people with an interest but no contacts or experience to get information about the voters in a particular area.

One of the methods of gathering information is by polling, which has been used at the Presidential level since the mid-1930's. Polls and pollsters have come a long way in accuracy since the Literary Digest poll that predicted Alfred Landon would beat Franklin D. Roosevelt in 1936. In the last ten years, political polling has spread to every level of the political system, with a sophistication that is difficult for the outsider to comprehend. Polls are now used to identify potential candidates, to decide whether or not to run, to test issue positions and advertising themes, and sometimes even to decide what to do in public office. They are still sometimes used to find out who is ahead, but that is now important only for fundraising (the money men like to see it on paper that their investment has a chance of paying off) and publicity.

Professional firms use a variety of polling techniques to help select candidates and to advise potential candidates about whether or not to run. One of the most frequently used is the name recognition poll in which the interviewer hands a voter a list of names and asks him how many he can identify. Included on the list are several potential candidates, the incumbent, other elected officials and perhaps some local celebrity or leader who could be convinced to run on the basis of wide favorable recognition.

One group of New Yorkers started their 1970 efforts with a poll. The Democratic leaders and money men, desperate to get rid of Rockefeller, did a general issue and name recognition poll late in 1969. They wanted to find a possible candidate able to beat Rockefeller, to convince him to run and to convince other potential candidates to stay out of the race. They tested the recognition and favorable image rating of several potential Democratic candidates for governor, and did "test runs" of elections with each of the possible candidates pitted against Rockefeller. The usual question was: If the election were being held today, which of these would you probably vote for—the Republican Rockefeller or the Democrat Goldberg (or another Democrat). From the poll, Arthur Goldberg emerged as one of the most respected and well-known men in the state.

If the election were held then, the poll indicated, Goldberg would defeat Rockefeller. Of course, the election was not being held then. Before it actually took place, Rockefeller would spend ten to fifteen million dollars pacifying the voters. The leaders ignored that ugly potential reality. They wanted a strong candidate and their poll told them Goldberg started out way ahead. Unfortunately for them and him, they convinced Goldberg to run. Goldberg narrowly won a primary against Howard Samuels and lost badly to a professional and expensive Rockefeller campaign in the general election.

In addition to name recognition polls, professional managers have polling techniques that assess the voters' image of the ideal candidate. Once they have the voters' idea of the ideal senator, governor or dogcatcher, the professionals can find out how closely their client meets it. They often make recommendations about how he can move closer to the ideal point. The device most frequently used for this kind of research is the semantic differential. The voter is given a set of opposite characteristics: bad/good, honest/dishonest, outgoing/reserved, *etc.* On a scale between each of these opposites he is asked to rank his ideal candidate and the incumbent or challenger. The answers are combined to form a composite picture of the ideal and actual candidates. Managers use the information to develop communications strategies that will move the image of their candidate closer to the ideal point.

Walter DeVries uses a form of the semantic differential to predict how undecided voters will actually cast their ballots. He combines the individual scales into three clusters: integrity, dynamism and competence. If a voter ranks a candidate well on two of the clusters, says DeVries, he will vote for the candidate.

Incumbents are being urged by the professionals to do this kind of research more than a year before their re-election campaigns. If the pollsters diagnose a problem, the official can change his behavior to come closer to the ideal and thus have a better chance of winning re-election.

Finding the voters' view of the real and ideal candidates is only part of the problem. The great majority of big campaigns for statewide or Congressional office now do at least one basic issue poll. The standard format for a complete public opinion survey includes personal interviews with about 400 probable voters. The interviewers get a great deal of background information about each voter and his or her views on a variety of public issues. The pollsters ask about the person's occupation, income, party, religion, education, and mark down the sex and race of each interviewee. Then they ask lots of questions about issues: Should the U.S. stay or get out of Vietnam? Should school children be bused? Should extra help be given to ghetto schools to help bring them up to high quality standards? Usually, there are several different questions about each major issue area to help the analysts judge how strongly the person feels about a particular issue. The reports given to candidates tell them at least two things: how many people feel a certain way on an issue and which people feel that way. For example, a poll can tell a candidate that 35 percent of his constituents are firmly opposed to busing, but they are all Republicans who are not going to vote for him no matter what he says about it.

The professional pollsters and campaign planners do not care about the substance of the issues or about what the people really think. They conduct issue polls to help find a vehicle for reaching the voter "at his right side." Opinion polling with socioeconomic breakdowns gives campaigners information about how they can get the interest of groups within the electorate that they want to reach during the campaign. The professional planners do not care whether it is the war or a new traffic light that is the burning issue. All they want is something around which to build a communication program and campaign theme.

Basic issue polls, which cost about $8,000 each, are often done eight months before the election. The results are sometimes checked during the course of the campaign with shorter telephone polls that ask a few key questions. A phone poll costs less than half as much as a field survey.

The election men also do research to test the effectiveness

of campaign themes, issue positions and advertisements they create, in the same way soaps and cereals are test-marketed. Small groups from the target audience are invited in to see a film or commercial and after it is over they discuss their reactions. From this in-depth response, the campaign planners learn how well their intended message is getting across.

The 1972 Nixon campaign started formally testing some campaign themes in late 1971. The professional managers used demographic and polling research to isolate target precincts that the President would need to carry to win re-election, and they started testing alternative themes and approaches in those districts. Many of the basic campaign decisions had been made more than a year before the election. Films, songs and printed material emphasizing "A generation of peace" had been produced by November, 1971, and they were being test-marketed around the country.

The opinion polls now being used by some candidates also include questions about the media habits of the voters. Once the polling and demographic research are combined to select the most likely supporters for a candidate, the media habit information is used to determine how to communicate with them and avoid wasting money on others who are either already convinced or lost to the opposition. For example, one of the reasons Governor William G. Milliken won re-election in Michigan in 1970 despite a strong sweep for the Democrats was the ability of his professional planners to target his advertising toward the undecided ticket-splitters. In September, 1970, they decided to use a magazine-type newspaper insert for their last big push rather than a 30-minute television show because their research showed that television advertising was not having much effect on the targeted ticket-splitters. Their polls indicated that the upper-income ticket-splitters paid more attention to newspapers. For lower-income ticket splitters, direct mail was recommended. The polls done for Milliken by DeVries also revealed that some possible voters listened to radio a great deal. As a result, the campaign added a modest radio advertising program geared around the stations and programs the undecided voters listened to.

Though polling research has become the basis of early campaign planning, many professionals continue to use polling throughout the campaign to monitor developments in issues and voter sentiments. While it is still quite expensive, an increasing number of professional campaign planners are using tracking surveys to follow the campaign. Constant telephone polling on a few questions allows campaign planners to judge the reactions to their efforts and to political events in general. For example, tracking surveys in Gary, Indiana, for Mayor Hatcher's re-election primary showed his campaign managers that he had an untapped reservoir of support among black youths. Earlier in the campaign, the strategists had concluded that he was weak among the younger voters and no special efforts were made for that vote. As a result of the tracking polls, a special late effort was made to get young people to the polls.

DeVries used extensive tracking for Milliken, too. In September and October, 1970, more than 6,000 telephone calls were made. They showed that in Kalamazoo and Traverse City, water pollution was a big issue, while crime and drugs were big in Detroit. Armed with this information, the media planners emphasized the pollution advertising spots in Kalamazoo and the drug and crime spots in Flint.

Matt Reese often tells potential clients that when you want to pick cherries, "You go where the cherries is," and when you want to get votes, you go where your voters are. You find them with demographic research. Studying past voting behavior is as important as polling to many campaign planners. Virtually all political scientists and politicians agree that the way a person voted in the past is a very good clue as to how he will vote in the future. Further, they believe that voters can be identified in relatively big groups whose behavior can be predicted. Professional campaign planners and political scientists do extensive demographic research to find how people in an area behaved in the past and to find easily identifiable characteristics that will help explain this behavior.

By correlating past behavior with political and socio-economic characteristics, they make generalizations about how certain types of voters will behave. Some of the most widely-known notions about voter behavior grew from this kind of research: rich people vote Republican, Catholic union members tend to vote Democratic, WASP's tend to be slightly more Republican, Jews are overwhelmingly Democratic. These broad demographic generalizations are enough for introductory students, but they are not nearly refined enough to plan a campaign in a particular Congressional district or state. Sophisticated professional campaign planners now do demographic research down to the individual precinct level, about 400 to 1,000 voters. Relatively simple computer programs make it possible to review and order an enormous amount of information about past behavior and social characteristics very quickly. Planners can now make distinctions about the probable voting behavior in every neighborhood or precinct that they look at.

Planners have two goals for demographic research: they want to know where the voters who supported this candidate or his party live and they want to know enough about them to find some more of the same type elsewhere in the district. Most of the campaign managers use rather standard political and socio-economic indicators to look for voting correlates. These include income, occupation, home ownership, education, race, religion, and political party. Information about all these characteristics is easily available from census reports or local election officials. A few campaign planners have invented their own characteristics to help them find the voters they need. For example Vincent Barabba, one of the best researchers in the business, has found that membership in the Brownies is often the best predictive variable he can find in the areas in which he usually runs campaigns. Parents who have little girls in the Brownies are precisely the kind of people who will vote for our Republican candidates, says Barabba.

DeVries has made almost a religion out of the concept of ticket-splitting. A great amount of his demographic and polling research is designed to identify the voters who split their tickets in an election, even though they may call themselves members of a political party. DeVries—and many others— think the ticket-splitters decide most elections and he wants his candidates to know where they are, what kind of people they are and how they can be effectively approached. He studies past returns, precinct by precinct, to find the voters who have moved back and forth across party lines in the same election. Once he finds where they are, he does demographic and polling research to determine what kind of people they are. These geographic and socio-economic groups become the targets for virtually all of the campaign activities.

Demographic research and public opinion polling have become so pervasive in political campaigning that no self-respecting candidate likes to be without his own poll, even if he does not know how to read the results or use the information. Almost every pollster and professional manager in the country has at least one story about a candidate who bought a poll, kept it prominently placed on his desk—or locked away in a drawer he could point to—just to show he was running a "modern" campaign. These candidates never read or use the polls they buy.

Good professional campaign managers do use their research as a base for writing formal strategic and operational campaign plans. Reese believes that both early research and early planning are keys to success in the new politics. He complains that too many campaigns are guided by the "Why don't we . . ." syndrome in which one genius after another comes along with a suggestion about what to do. Elections scheduled for November should be planned long before, according to Reese. That way, candidates can get "result-measured management" for their investments.

Reese wrote the basic campaign plan for one candidate for governor in 1972, delivering it in July, 1971, 16 months before the election. It was about 300 pages long and it told the candidate what he had to do to get ready to campaign and how to do it. The preliminary plan recognized that the candidate had many advantages including vast financial resources, great popularity and an attractive reform record, and provided for a way to manage all these resources carefully to prevent any of them from being dissipated.

The general strategy for the period was to have the candidate continue to develop his popularity by speaking out in favor of the various reform measures he advocated for the state. He would continue serving in his present office and not talk much about a possible race for governor. In the meantime, he would build his campaign organization, creating an independent statewide citizens' movement, ostensibly to convince the candidate to run and to emphasize his independent reformist stands. After he finally announced, the citizens' movement would become the principal campaign organization. The plan outlined how the movement should be organized and staffed, how county leaders and regular members would be recruited and a step-by-step program for building an organization in each county in the state.

While the candidate was to use his reform stands and his independence as organizing tools for the campaign, the plan warned him against alienating the regular party forces in the state. To prevent that, the plan suggested how the candidate could organize his own staff and activities to keep in close touch with the regular party leadership.

Finally, the plan outlined the staff needs of the candidate, gave him a table of organization to enable his director of operations to keep control over both the citizens' movement and the continuing contact with the regular party, and told him what kind of specific issue research he needed for each county in the state. The plan was supplemented by sample forms of all sorts, including draft letters to potential citizens' movement county chairmen, telephone instructions and political intelligence and press monitoring forms. The candidate swamped his opposition in the Spring, 1972 primary.

When Richard S. Schweiker decided to run for the Senate from Pennsylvania in 1968, his campaign consultants gave him a plan, too. The men who prepared the campaign plan, Douglas Bailey, John Deardourff and David Goldberg, traveled to the state regularly during the campaign to consult on its implementation. The campaign plan was delivered in May, 1968, and covered every day up to Election Day.

Schweiker's campaign planners told him there were three strategic considerations. First, polling research showed that few people outside his Congressional District knew who he was or had much of an idea about what kind of person he was. Second, demographic research showed that he would have to persuade some normally Democratic voters to vote for him. Third, he would have to retain a flexible approach until it was clear who the Republican Presidential nominee would be.

The planners divided the campaign into three major periods. The first, from May to August, would concentrate on solving the candidate's name recognition problems. The professional planners told Schweiker to spend $161,000 on billboards, newspapers and direct mail advertising to make his name a household word in Pennsylvania. During August, the professional planners recommended that he conduct a relatively low profile campaign among Republicans while he waited to see who the Presidential nominee would be and what difference that would make for his own plans. From Labor Day on, the candidate would concentrate on a hard sell to convince the swing voters to go for him. The hard sell portion of the campaign would rely heavily on television advertising.

Schweiker was told that he should emphasize issues but that his positions need not be different from the incumbent's. Rather than argue with Senator Joseph Clark, they suggested that Schweiker talk about issues in order to demonstrate his practicality, youthfulness and ability to serve. They recommended that he talk about his own plan to end the war, draft reform and some urban issue, probably education.

The campaign plan gave Schweiker a complete table of organization, three alternative budgets ranging from $500,000 to $1,000,000, a recommended polling schedule and a complete vote history analysis of the state for use in scheduling advertising and appearance priorities. On the basis of past voting behavior, the planners established target areas for the candidate in different parts of the state, allocating his advertising and personal appearance schedules on the basis of the areas they thought would be most important to his victory. In short, they designed a schedule that had him spend most of his time and most of his money in the few areas that would produce most of his votes.

In September, after the Republican and Democratic National Conventions, the consultants wrote a supplementary report that analyzed the impact of the Nixon and Humphrey campaigns on Schweiker's chances. The candidate was told to endorse Nixon warmly and it was suggested that the basic issue in the campaign should be "something is wrong with our political process." A basic text for the candidate to use to emphasize the theme was included.

In addition to research and planning, the Reese firm accepts operational responsibility for portions of the campaign, too. Reese specializes in voter registration, precinct organization and other activity-producing things. He uses his own people and his own manuals of procedure to register target voters or mobilize thousands of volunteers for a candidate. Bailey, Deardourff and Bowen concentrates on planning and executing the advertising portions of the campaign plans they write. They know that advertising is where the money can be made in modern campaigns. As the advertising agency, they are usually entitled to a 15 percent commission on all the time the candidate buys and a normal profit mark-up on the production costs of the advertising. In a million dollar advertising campaign, that can add up to more than $200,000.

While most firms like to be involved in many campaigns at the same time, they are almost always in different geographic areas. The companies work for individual candidates, each on his own. The election season is now marked by dozens of mini-wars, planned, managed and fought by small teams. The candidates for each office face off as if they were the only contest. As a result, they compete not only with each other, but with the candidates in all the other mini-wars in their area for the time and attention of the voters.

The party labels candidates wear have little importance for the campaign. They are just one element among many that the professional planners keep in mind. Sometimes the party level is to emphasized and at other times hidden. When Goldwater was the Republican candidate for President in 1964, DeVries recommended that his Republican clients in Michigan run as independent-minded individuals, trying to ignore their party label. Two years later, he told the same people to run as regular Republicans proud of their party. In the professional campaigns of the 1970's, the political party is a tool in a campaign, not the basis of politics.

Turning responsibility for managing an election over to a group of "outsiders" is a marked departure from the tradition of American politics where party loyalty has always been more important than competence. But that is exactly what happened in 1970 throughout the country and it is exactly what Whitaker and Baxter had in mind when they set up Campaigns Inc. in 1934.

CHAPTER 4

How It All Began

We can't beat state socialism in this country by running away from controversy; we have to meet it head on, in an open contest before the people. Negative victories aren't enough either; we have to do a dynamic job of selling American fundamentals.

> —*Clem Whitaker Sr., partner in the first campaign management firm, in a speech to the second annual meeting of the Public Relations Society, New York, December, 1949.*

Something hit us like a ton of transistors. We found that the lives of the people . . . today were no longer affected by the sounds of their immediate environment. Their lives are now primarily affected by sounds of a much, much larger world reaching them via radio, television, records, tapes and telephone.

> —*Tony Schwartz, president of a firm that produces radio and sound for television campaign advertising, in an article in* Communication Arts *in 1969.*

Someday we'll elect a Republican President who is worth electing. In the meantime we'll make lots of money.

> —*A Republican professional campaign manager in 1969.*

These very different remarks go a long way toward explaining why professional campaign managers have appeared in American politics. Traditional political elites, fearing things were collapsing around them, looked for a way to keep their hold on public power and policy. The whole environment in which politics was conducted was changing. Professional campaign management firms were a satisfactory response to the new environment of politics.

Like so many other 20th century developments, professional campaign management was born in California. Whitaker and Baxter, founded in 1934, was the first firm and it served as a model of power and profitability for the industry. For almost 20 years, Clem Whitaker Sr. and his wife and partner, Leone Baxter, were the undisputed political "bosses" of California Republicans. Whitaker denied that they were political bosses and wrote that if nominated for the job, ". . . we would decline with absolute finality." Whitaker and Baxter, of course, were not political bosses in the traditional sense, but then traditions die easily in California. They were political bosses in the new and modern sense. Old bosses could deliver voters to candidates because of their access to them through precinct captains. Whitaker and Baxter and many of the new political bosses delivered voters because of their access to them through research and the mass media. When Whitaker and Baxter got started, the mass media still meant newspapers; they built a statewide network of connections with all the newspapers, especially the relatively small weekly papers, which they used with great skill throughout the year to plug the interests and values of their clients and candidates.

Whitaker and Baxter used the tools of mass democracy and mass communication to protect the interests of the oil companies, utilities, railroads, doctors (they conducted the American Medical Association's campaign against national health insurance in 1948) and other representatives of the "American way" who could pay their fees. They gave their clients a method of taking the offensive in politics; they showed businessmen and doctors that they need not be defensive. In the process, Whitaker and Baxter became the people to see in California politics.

Whitaker probably learned about politics from his job as a political reporter in Sacramento and about people from his

Baptist preacher father. He showed his talent as a writer and communicator early in his life. By the time he was 19 he was city editor of the Sacramento *Union*. Soon after that, he opened a news bureau that distributed articles about state politics to local and daily papers throughout California. His Capitol News Bureau was a success, but he sold it for health reasons.

In the early 1930's he decided to combine his writing and preaching background—and went into public relations. He brought with him a belief that a simple theme, repeated frequently and dramatically over the right channels, would carry a long way. One of his first clients was a group of barbers concerned about pending legislation requiring barbers to register. Whitaker decided not to deal with the legislators directly. He knew that each legislator had a barber of his own and many more in his district. He got the barbers to write their own state legislators, and to bend their ears about the legislation while shaving carefully around them. It was subtle, but it worked, and Whitaker had his razor's edge of organization and communication—go to the people affected and give them a simple theme to repeat.

In 1933, Whitaker became associated with the efforts to defeat a popular referendum on the Central Valley electric project and he met Leone Baxter, who was working for the Redding Chamber of Commerce and who was regarded as a shrewd political tactician. Whitaker and Baxter met in the Sacramento law office of Sheridan Downey, who suggested that they get together and manage the campaign to defeat the project. They formed Campaigns, Inc. for the purpose and won. Downey's feeling that they would make a good team was accurate. They decided to stay in the campaign business--and to get married.

One of its first efforts in 1934 was against Upton Sinclair and his "End Poverty in California" (EPIC) movement, a depression-born mass movement of the poor and unemployed. Sinclair, its organizer and spokesman, ran for governor against the "interests" in 1934. The "interests" were scared and they wanted him beaten. Sinclair had the mass movement but business had money and the organizing and communicating skills of Whitaker and Baxter.

Leone Baxter's glass-walled penthouse in San Francisco's Fairmont Hotel in 1969 was dominated by a huge modern religious sculpture. She and her husband always liked to emphasize a moral or religious tone in their candidates. Perhaps that is why she described her firm's role in defeating Sinclair as something approaching an act of grace:

> It wasn't that we were for Merriam (Sinclair's opponent). We didn't think he'd make much of a governor and we wouldn't campaign for him . . . And we liked Sinclair as a person. But it would have been a disaster if he had been elected. He couldn't possibly have carried through on all the wild promises he had made. Probably he would have been shot by his own supporters.

Between 1934 and 1958, Whitaker and Baxter planned and ran about 75 major political campaigns, and won 90 percent of them. They brought order and predictability in California politics to those who could pay for it. Their clients included most major Republican candidates, including Earl Warren in his first gubernatorial campaign, Pacific Gas and Electric, the American Medical Association, the major railroads, and 40 large agricultural producers in California.

They operated through several subsidiary companies. Whitaker and Baxter or Campaigns, Inc., would plan and manage the campaign from start to finish for a fee that Whitaker liked to call "prideful"—others would call it large. They also operated a full advertising agency, the Clem Whitaker Advertising Agency, which placed all the advertising for their campaigns and kept the standard 15 percent agency fee. Their statewide organization and contacts were maintained year-round through a third company, the California Features Service, which they began in 1936. The service was a general and political news bureau that provided boiler-plate copy (articles and other items ready for insertion into a newspaper without change) to the 700 daily and weekly papers then published in California. The articles distributed through the California Features Service often promoted the views of the corporate clients and candidates who were paying fees to Whitaker and Baxter or Campaigns, Inc. During campaigns, the Whitaker Advertising Agency placed advertising for its political candidates in the papers using the California Features Service without taking the usual 15 percent commission. Whitaker and Baxter, and the views they were hired to promote, were almost always welcome friends in the publishers' offices of California newspapers.

Whitaker and Baxter had supreme confidence in their own ability and methods and an open contempt for traditional political organization. Whitaker argued that before they came along campaigns had been the "natural province of broken-down politicians and alcoholic camp followers." When a candidate or client went through their door for help, Whitaker and Baxter became the boss. The client paid the bills and did what Whitaker and Baxter told him to do, at least for the duration of the campaign. They would start by doing prodigious research on the client, on the opposition and on the possible issues. Their preliminary research on a campaign might be as long as a million words. The two partners would take that bulk of information and reduce it to a strategy revolving around a simple theme.

The Whitakers believed in drama so they would withdraw into semi-seclusion for the strategy and theme-writing period. When they emerged, they had a theme and a plan for the campaign that had to be followed as if they were written on stone. They would also try game strategy for the opposition to plan ways they would react. The companies controlled by the couple did everything for the campaign—they hired, organized and directed the field staff; they created, wrote and placed the advertising and literature; they set up the candidate's schedule and gave him things to say when he got where they sent him; they mobilized what they thought to be the relevant special interest groups and volunteers and provided them with ammunition for the campaign; and Whitaker and Baxter controlled all the money. All the candidate had to do was have the total amount in by Election Day. At times, they advanced campaigns tens of thousands of dollars of their own. Other campaigns would have had to shut down until the money arrived, but that did not happen with Whitaker and Baxter.

Like all politicians, they made many friends and many enemies. Their dominance of California Republican politics ended in 1958 when they got caught in the middle of an internal Republican battle. It was the year of the big switch in California, with Goodwin Knight, the incumbent Republican governor, running for the Senate while William Knowland, the incumbent Republican U.S. Senator, came home and ran for governor. The Whitakers had managed Knight's first campaign for governor. He wanted to run again in 1958 and they supported him. But Southern Californians, led by then Vice President Nixon, insisted that Knight run for the Senate and Knowland for governor so Knowland could start building a national political base.

Whitaker and Baxter were active participants in the battle, but lost. When the election was over, the Democrats were in power in Sacramento for the first time in many many years and Whitaker and Baxter were out of power in the Republican Party. They sold the state politics part of the business to their son, Clem Jr., who continues to operate a highly-successful political public relations and campaign management business but it no longer has a monopoly or even a dominant position in California. Clem Whitaker Sr. and Leone Baxter formed Whitaker and Baxter International in 1965 and continued to counsel corporate clients. Clem Sr. died but Leone Baxter continued to be an active political consultant throughout the 1960's.

Whitaker and Baxter was formed at the encouragement

of leaders of the traditional business and political elite of California, which felt its dominance threatened by events and changes going on around it. The firm succeeded and survived because it adapted to the structural and environmental changes taking place. For many years, Whitaker and Baxter was the only professional campaign management firm. The partners were delighted that they had found a business in which there was virtually no competition. However, Whitaker and Baxter was no aberration.

From its start in 1934, the campaign management industry grew rather slowly. A few companies went in and out of business shortly after World War II, and some public relations and advertising firms started accepting political campaign clients in the late 1940's. During the 1950's there was a slow but steady expansion. It is in the last ten years, however, that the industry has exploded into our midst and consciousness. By every possible measure, the recent growth of the professional campaign management industry has been remarkable. The number of firms, the geographic areas in which they regularly work, the level of politics at which they sell their services and the sheer number of campaigns in which they are involved have all been accelerating rapidly.

Only partial comparisons with the state of the industry in the 1950's are possible because almost no one paid attention to the emerging industry. However, enough information is available to show very rapid growth in the 1960's.

For example, Alexander Heard found 41 public relations firms that said they offered complete campaign management services in 1957. In 1972, there were close to 100 such firms. All of the firms Heard reported on were public relations companies that did campaigns as only part of their business. In 1972, there were about 60 firms that called themselves professional campaign management firms and did the bulk of their business in political campaigns. In addition, there were at least 200 other companies around the country offering professional campaign management services as part of their business.

More than half the firms Heard reported on were located

in California, New York, and Texas, working on campaigns in only a few states. In 1960, professional campaign managers were working in fewer than ten states on a regular basis. Today, professional management firms have worked in elections in every state in the union and can be regularly found at work on elections at all levels in more than thirty states. (The test of regularity used here is evidence that professional managers have worked in at least two elections at five of the six electoral levels, President through mayor, that were examined.)

The firms that cooperated with this study supplied information on 2,292 campaigns in which they worked during the 1960's. The following table shows the phenomenal increases that have occurred at all levels of the electoral system since a similar cycle in our electoral pattern was studied in the 1950's.

The percent increase in campaign management services comparing 1952–1957* and 1964–1969.**

	Any professional service in the primary	Any professional service in the general	Full campaign management service
U.S. President***	359%	200%	622%
U.S. Senate	405	505	722
U.S. Representative	371	575	842
Statewide races	151	219	626
Local	145	159	298

* As reported by Alexander Heard in *The Costs of Democracy* (1960) p. 417, of the 130 public relations firms participating, 41 offered full campaign management services.

** 143 firms reported their campaign activities for this period; 71 said they offered full campaign management services.

*** A firm is often involved in one state for a Presidential campaign. Many firms report working in the same election but in different states.

The growth in participation in Presidential primaries may be explained by the growth in the number of primaries. Based on what happened in 1972 it may be possible to argue that the availability of professional campaign managers is actually encouraging such primaries. The Wilbur Mills and John Lindsay campaigns were made possible by professional media and direct mail companies. If these services had not been available for hire neither of these candidates could have seriously thought about running for President. The rest of the growth is also remarkable. Firms reported twice as much involvement in Presidential general elections and statewide races during the 1960's as in the 1950's. At the Congressional level, firms reported five times as much activity in Senate general elections and almost six times as much in the House general elections during the 1960's. Reported activity at the local level increased by about 50 percent. In the 1970's the growth rate has remained about the same.

The sophistication of services offered to campaigns by professional firms also grew dramatically over the comparable periods. This is particularly true in the area of full campaign management, from the start to the finish of a campaign. Full management was offered more than eight times more frequently for House races in the 1960's than in the 1950's.

More impressive than the rate of growth over the 15-year period is the rate at which it has been accelerating, with 40 percent of all the campaigns reported during the 1960's taking place in 1968 and 1969. The diagram on page 53 shows the growth.

The figures for 1969 also show the attempts of the firms to make campaign management a continuing rather than a seasonal business; 10 percent of all the campaign services reported for the decade were given in a year when there were very few big elections. This figure reflects the spread of the industry into the lower electoral levels and the increasing ability of the professional management firms to get contracts to plan campaigns more than a year before the election date.

Number of campaigns in which professional services were provided 1960–1970. (143 firms reported activities during this period.)

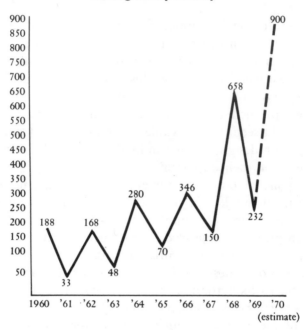

While complete figures for 1971 are not available, it is evident that this trend has accelerated. Virtually all the firms had at least some campaign work in 1971.

The exact figures for 1970 elections are not available. The estimate, based on interviews and newspaper accounts, shows the curve continuing to rise sharply. It was the year of the professional campaign manager. Professional management companies provided services of one kind or another to both sides of virtually every contested Senate and gubernatorial election and to the bulk of the primary contests as well. In some campaigns, as many as three or four firms provided different services. In addition, the professional firms were hired to work in at least 150 House of Representative contests and probably in more than 300 state legislative races. The professional managers were active in more campaigns in 1970 than ever before, even though there was no Presidential election.

The professional campaign management industry has grown from one firm operating in one state in the 1930's to several hundred firms operating in most states at all electoral levels. If we were to examine this development purely from the perspective of our traditional notion that election campaigns are planned and organized by political parties, this invasion would seem unbelievable. This growth did not occur by stealth or design; rather, individuals around the country saw and seized their opportunity.

Most political observers believe the political parties have become much weaker in the last 25 years. It is tempting to draw a simple line of causality to suggest that professional campaign managers appeared on the scene because our traditional political party structures collapsed. That's too simple and raises more questions than answers. It is more accurate and useful to look for reasons in the social environment of political organization and communication.

One of the reasons frequently given for both the decline of parties and the rise of professional campaign managers relates to structural or institutional changes we have made in the way we conduct our politics, especially the introduction of the direct primary. Maurice Duverger and others have argued that the direct primary contributed to the weakening of American political parties and thus to the emergence of new kinds of organizations to organize and fight election contests. Indeed, the people who first dreamed up the idea of direct primaries to choose nominees for public office—the Progressives—wanted to use the device to break the back of the party machines.

The introduction of the primary and popular referendum has been used by some to explain why management firms developed first in California. As one manager put it: "It's all those silly laws Hiram Johnson had passed. The candidates have to go someplace for the primary." During Johnson's administration, the electoral laws of the state were completely rewritten. Direct primaries were introduced and political parties were prohibited from endorsing or helping candidates before the primary. Candidates were allowed to enter the primaries of several parties at the same time. Johnson and his supporters also had relatively permissive popular referenda provisions enacted. To top it off, all elections in California below the level of state legislature were made non-partisan. In this manner, Johnson destroyed all the political party organizations, except his own. When he retired to the U.S. Senate in 1916, he left something of a political vacuum which new organizational forms have been rushing to fill ever since. California has been host to both mass movements like EPIC, the California Republican Assembly and the California Democratic caucus and to elite political management firms like Whitaker and Baxter.

Carey McWilliams's explanation for the development of professional campaign managers in California tacitly accepts the structural approach outlined above:

> The basic explanation for "professionalism" in California politics is to be found in the state's penchant for direct legislation . . . the people keep putting measures on the ballot and the "interests" keep defeating them—or most of them.

The structural argument for the emergence of professional campaign management firms suggests that legal changes in the electoral system and state regulation of political parties weakened parties and allowed professional campaign management firms to take over many of their electoral functions. This is a clean line of causality, but it rests on false assumptions and may well mask far more than it reveals about the changes taking place in American politics and about the emergence of a new political elite.

First, the argument assumes that political parties were very strong before the reformers started changing the rules. There were successful urban political machines with working precinct organizations and effective ties to business and religious elites. However, we have probably mythologized their strengths beyond recognition and, more seriously, we have assumed they existed all over the country. In fact, effective political machine organizations never existed simultaneously all over the country. They were essentially local affairs concerned with local offices and their rewards. Statewide and national electoral politics have always been more loosely organized. Some analysts believe the American national party organizations reached their highest levels of organization and strength in the late 1820's when Martin Van Buren organized the Democratic Party for Jackson's and his own election to the Presidency. Further, the landed gentry Democrats managed to control politics in the South for almost a hundred years without developing much local or precinct organization. They just did not let many blacks or poor whites vote. In the South, there has not been a decline of parties; rather, there has been the absence of parties in any real sense.

It is true that the strong party organizations that dominated politics in some American cities are now gone. (Except in Chicago and Albany where the old organizations have recently whipped some of the professional campaign management firms.) Legal changes such as the introduction of civil service, party primaries and non-partisan local elections contributed to their decline. But these changes did not really "cause" the parties to decline. Rather, they were themselves reflections of other more fundamental changes that were occurring in the atmosphere of politics.

The Progressives did not succeed in destroying parties, but they did leave behind a stench that has hung over political parties and politics. For example, Samuel Hays has argued that a substantial portion of the industrialized elites of the

Progressive period (roughly 1880–1920) viewed political parties as the bulwark of resistance to modernization and change. That view continues today among many elements in the population. Political parties are alternately viewed as powerless but annoying bags of wind or evil groups dedicated to preventing the will of the people to be exercised in nominations, elections or public policy. In public opinion polls, parties are our least respected political institution.

There is a second reason the simple line from decline of party to emergence of professional managers cannot be followed. The sequence of cause and effect is not clear. Further, the structural changes that were alleged to be the cause were made many years ago and professional management is quite new. Rather than structural changes causing management firms to appear, the reverse may be true, in fact. Professional management may be among the causes of recent changes in structural arrangements, like direct primaries. In 1971, both the Alaska and Florida legislatures passed bills enacting early Presidential primaries, one of the arguments being the boost they would give to the economy. The professional managers, it was argued, would spend fortunes in the states on polls, staff, hotels, rented cars, and offices and media advertising. The Republican governor of Alaska vetoed the early primary, probably under some pressure from the White House. The Democratic governor of Florida signed the bill for an early primary and he watched the candidates and the followers add more than ten million dollars to his state's economy.

Finally, the structural argument does not fully explain what happened because it does not shed light on why private profit-making campaign management firms have emerged as a response to the changes. On the face of it, other responses could have been as likely. For example, why didn't the structural changes produce the Progressives' goal of direct mass politics? Why didn't the mass membership type organizations that emerged in California last or spread to the rest of the country? Campaign management firms are just one possible alternative to traditional campaign organization, but they are the one that has spread throughout the system.

Other factors help explain more about both the decline of political parties and the rise of professional campaign management firms. They are at once obvious and profound.

The greatest change that has taken place in the political environment has been the number of people who vote: 49,900,000 voted for President in 1940; 73,211,562 did so in 1968. This is a 47 percent increase in only 28 years and it is accounted for almost completely by growth in the total population. The level of participation has stayed about the same; 59.8 percent of the eligible electorate voted in 1940 compared to 61 percent in 1968. If the percent of participation stayed steady in 1972, about 87,000,000 people will have voted for President, an increase of about 18 percent over 1968.

The population has changed in other central ways, too. It is incredibly mobile. One fifth of us—more than 40 million people—move every year, a migration of historic proportions. Many professional managers do not bother to keep computer voter lists from one election to the next because more than 40 percent of the names or addresses will change. This almost frenetic movement makes traditional precinct organization virtually impossible at a cost most parties can afford to pay. About the only thing some leaders can hope for is one-time involvement.

These massive changes have been particularly exaggerated in California. That state's rate of growth has been two to six times greater than the national average for 60 years. Californians have also urbanized and suburbanized more completely and quickly than the rest of us. The people in California seem to move around faster than the cars on their freeway. By 1950, 80.7 percent of California residents had moved to urban-suburban areas while the national figure was 64 percent. In 1970, California was still ahead but the gap was much smaller.

A second major change has been the shift from print to sight and sound communications. In 1946, there were 7,000 television sets in the country; in 1972, nearly 90 million television sets. The vast majority of Americans now get the bulk of their political information from television and radio. And, the first generation to grow up watching television has now entered the electorate.

Radio and television have changed political communication in two fundamental ways. First, television gives us at least vicarious experience with the whole world; our sight and sound perspective is now worldwide. We are no longer limited to what we can see, touch or smell with our own faculties. Our local environment, the base of traditional political organization, is no longer the focus of our attention. Television has accelerated the nationalization of politics that has marked much of the 20th century.

Television has done something else; it has made most of us illiterate again. We can all receive communication from radio and television, but very few of us know how to produce communication for transmission to others. We can read but not write. The politicians have been very sensitive to this new reality and have generally been afraid of television. Professional campaign managers claim they have the skills of modern communication and can put them at the disposal of candidates. They have been showing the politicians how to use communication and research to win.

To recognize that television has had a profound effect on our political communication patterns does not say anything about the way professional managers use television advertising in campaigns. Television, as a medium of communication, may have tremendous impact on us while political advertising on television may have very little impact. The Texas election in 1970 perhaps is a case in point. Texas was an important target state for the Republicans, who believed they could capture both the U.S. Senate seat and the governor's mansion. The Republicans fielded attractive and experienced candidates, George Bush for the Senate and Paul Eggers for governor. The candidates were well supplied with money and professional campaign management. Their campaigns were also blessed with an almost continuous airlift of Cabinet members, Republican Congressional leaders, the Vice President and even the President himself. The message brought by all these VIP's was that the election in Texas was crucial for the nation and that the President needed George Bush in the Senate to help get his programs through. The participation of so many members of the Cabinet and of the President himself in mid-term elections was unprecedented. The traveling road-show was very heavily covered by television news, nationally almost every night and locally wherever the high-level officials stopped. The President's visit to Texas the weekend before the election was especially well covered on television. In addition, both the Republicans and Democrats ran election-eve national broadcasts stressing the importance of the elections.

On Election Day the voters of Texas behaved the way they have for a hundred years; they elected Democrats to the Senate and the governor's mansion, though their margins of victory were small. The only difference between 1970 and other mid-term elections in Texas was that slightly more people actually went to the polls than had been expected from past experience. It is reasonable to suggest that television news coverage of the election, especially all those national leaders coming to Texas to say how important the election was, increased interest and thus turnout in the election. The planned, paid television advertising for the candidates amounting to more than one million dollars probably had almost no impact on this phenomenon.

If this argument is correct, the Republicans killed themselves with love and help in Texas and perhaps in other places in 1970. Had fewer people voted, the Republicans might well have won in Texas. In fact, low turnout was the principal goal of the Republican gubernatorial candidate's managers.

They thought they could get a million votes; they actually got 1,037,723, which would have been enough if the expected two million people voted. They were beaten by the larger than expected turnout of 2,231,667, about 10 percent more than predicted. They openly blamed the big turnout on the interest stirred up by all the out-of-state visitors and by the popular referendum authorizing liquor by the drink.

The traditional forms of political organization simply could not cope with massive changes. Suddenly there were too many voters who were constantly on the move, and who got their information about politics sealed in their living rooms watching a screen over which the local party leader had no influence and about their governmental services from career civil service bureaucrats. There was less community base on which to build political organization.

The political atmosphere has changed in yet another crucial way. The feeling and fact of growing social insecurity (easily measured by indices of war, crime, civil unrest, rapid inflation or high unemployment) has been another reason professional campaign management firms have emerged. Lasswell has shown that a shift of business expenditures from regular commercial advertising to political propaganda paralleled the rise of political and social instability that preceded the Nazi takeover in Germany in the 1930's. He argued that groups that felt threatened by what was going on in the society began investing heavily in political parties and propaganda to try to get a more stable situation or at least to protect themselves (in fact their activities often contributed to the instability around them). Lasswell pointed out that the propagandists who had served the commercial interests of the companies shifted into political propaganda. That is what happended in California when Whitaker and Baxter were hired to lead the state's commercial interests into political battle with the "State Socialists."

Businessmen have always invested heavily in American politics. Through the first 30 years of the 20th century, business interests were well represented at the national level through their heavy contributions to the Republican Party, which usually controlled the White House. At the local level, most businesses had, and have, working relationships with the political powers.

In the 1930's, however, a new and different situation arose. The Democrats were in power in Washington and in many of the states, the machines were loosening up in the cities and the economy was in a vast depression. The political terrain had changed, and businessmen needed guidance to cope with the new situations. Workers were organizing in the shops and in the halls of the legislatures. The growth of government intervention in the economy was accompanied by a growth of intervention by business and labor in politics. For many industries, government policies have more effect on the profit and growth prospects of firms than the commercial actions the firms take. Large economic interests have needed advice on how to be successful in politics. When they could not get what they needed in the accustomed way, they turned to people who had helped them deal with the outside world, the public relations and advertising men.

Since 1960, civil unrest, opposition to the government, disaffection with the political system, crime, racial tension and fear, mostly fear, have all grown. The investment in politics by business and professional men and by well-established unions has escalated in parallel. In 1971, an astounding 47 percent of a nationwide sample expressed deep pessimism for the future of the country. As instability and fear have grown so have the political activities of large economic forces and institutions.

Professional managers have helped show them the way. The majority of America's largest corporations and unions have special departments or people designated to handle their public and political affairs. Additionally, most of the major corporations have special funds through which higher ranking executives contribute a small portion of their salaries for the political purposes of the company. A frequent arrangement is that all salaried employees who make more than $15,000 contribute one-half of 1 percent of their salary to the fund, which is administered by the officer in charge of the political relations of the company.

A study of corporate activities in politics released by the National Industrial Conference Board in 1968 showed that more than 500 companies had political education programs for their employees, some of them on a continuous basis. The majority of these programs have been initiated in recent years. The amount of political contributions that could be traced to business and union sources more than doubled during the 1960's.

Much of the increased business activity in politics has been channelled through professional campaign management firms in several ways. Some companies hire professional campaign management firms to give political education seminars to their employees. Other companies have used professional campaign management and public relations firms to serve as a conduit for illegal contributions from the corporations to campaigns. Several of the recent indictments and convictions for illegal corporate contributions to Federal campaigns resulted from Internal Revenue Service investigations of the books of campaign management and public relations firms in California. For example, National Breweries was indicted for making an illegal contribution to the campaign of Pierre Salinger in 1964 through a payment to Walter Leftwich and Associates, a political public relations firm in California.

Trade and professional associations have increased their direct political activities in recent years through the establishment of special political action funds. The American Medical Association Political Action Fund (AMPAC) was credited with having raised and contributed almost five million dollars to political campaigns in 1968. Professional campaign managers are central to this effort, too. AMPAC has had a continuing contract with at least one professional campaign management firm for political research and polls in districts where the association was promoting a candidate who would be friendly toward the political positions of the A.M.A. This type of contract helps firms meet their operating expenses between elections.

As large non-political institutions have moved into new political areas to protect or strengthen their positions, they have needed expanded and sophisticated political guidance. Professional campaign management firms have been a convenient and comfortable way to get the services they need.

Today, professional campaign management is so pervasive its practitioners cover the normal political spectrum. In fact there are more managers who classify themselves individually as liberals than as conservatives, but even they work closely with corporate interests.

Logically, the skills professional managers bring to political campaigns can be used to advocate social change and progressive positions as easily as any other. Thus, there is no inherent reason why the industry should be linked to conservative business-oriented causes or groups; there are only practical reasons.

First, businessmen had contact and experience with professional propagandists in their commercial ventures. They were also open to the idea of outside management and consulting help. Most of them had limited experience in politics and were not wedded to any organizational form or process. What they needed were results.

Second, businessmen and professionals, like doctors, had the cash it took to buy the professional's services and to pay for the campaigns they planned. Now, other groups have responded and they, too, have raised cash instead of other resources to pay for professional campaigns. The nine million dollars raised by the McCarthy campaign in 1968 and the six to eight million dollars regularly raised by union political funds show that liberals can raise money, too. Since the late 1950's, campaign spending has been doubling about every four years. A major part of the responsibility for this rise rests with the professional managers. It is the techniques they recommend that have driven up the cost of campaigning.

In summary, the emergence of the professional campaign management industry is just another clear indication that the political world around us is changing very rapidly. The people who set up professional management firms recognized those changes earlier than the rest of us and created a new organizational form that could adapt to them. The form they invented, private profit-making companies, is closely tied to the goals and motivations of the managers themselves.

CHAPTER 5

Where Did They Come From?

> But I'm a pro. I don't make mistakes.
> —*Matt Reese, talking about the Tate for Mayor primary.*

> He was a beautiful beautiful body, and we were selling sex.
> —*Robert Goodman, talking about Spiro Agnew's campaign for governor of Maryland in 1966.*

> Television is cotton candy. Politics is real.
> —*Robert Squier, talking about his work.*

Matt Reese and his colleagues are in a new industry and profession. Some of the practitioners of professional campaign management got into the business by printing stationery and getting a telephone listing. Others worked and planned at establishing their own firms. The 1970 elections notwithstanding, these men and women have convinced candidates for high and modest public office to entrust their political futures and fortunes to them.

It is fair to ask where the practitioners of this new industry came from. What were they doing before they set out to remake American politics for the television age? What kind of training do they have? What kinds of firms have they established? And finally, what is it that the professional managers want?

The United States is not a government of men, it is a government of lawyers. The elected offices and top executive positions in this country are almost totally dominated by lawyers. The men and women who run the campaigns, however, have completely different backgrounds. Lawyers do participate in campaigns, but they no longer dominate them. There is a growing gap between the views of the lawyers and of the men who actually run the campaigns, as was vividly shown in McGinniss's description of the 1968 Nixon campaign. The lawyers, like John Mitchell, clashed frequently with the modern managers, like Harry Treleaven. McGinniss recounts that Treleaven complained that he could feel control slipping out of the hands of the managers into the hands of the lawyers, who he thought did not understand modern campaigning.

The professional managers accept as natural a clash between them and their lawyer candidates. They do not expect lawyers to understand marketing. As one of the managers put it:

> Politics has nothing to do with running for office. When you run for office there is a product, the candidate, and people who buy the product. It's a market and you can get a list of all the customers, the registered voters. The dumbbells in politics don't understand this.

Because it is so new, there is no well-defined route to becoming a professional manager. However, there are several ways to learn how to do the things the professional campaign managers do in campaigns. The industry is a mélange of people with backgrounds in communications arts, politics and behavioral or marketing research.

The majority of the professional managers who cooperated with this study had training and experience in communications—36 percent came from public relations, 15 percent from journalism, 10 percent from advertising and 6 percent from radio and television. Like the originators of the industry, Whitaker and Baxter, they make their special claims to power in elections on the basis of their skills as communicators to a large and mobile population.

Journalism has been a popular breeding ground for both public relations and professional campaign management ever since Ivy Lee opened the first private publicity bureau and Charles Michaelson left the Hearst papers to head a newly-created publicity department in the Democratic National Committee. Print journalists were the country's first mass communicators. Those who went into public relations and politics were more likely to have been "guys" from the mass circulation sheets, like the Hearst papers, than to have been "gentlemen" from the *Times*.

The public relations approach in business tells clients to take their case "to the people" and to present their side of any story on their own terms. Public relations men have been very successful in selling both their approach and themselves to American organizations. Almost every American corporation, large civic association and governmental agency has public relations men at a high decision-making level. The long-term public relations effort of A.T.&T. has been so successful that many people still ring the praises of "Ma Bell" even though the telephones themselves stopped ringing reliably several years ago.

The application of public relations to politics has been similar. It was accurately characterized by Richard Harris, when he described the reasons Otis Pike's campaign managers refused to use public relations men in their campaigns for the House of Representatives:

> Basically the public relations approach is different. . . .
> The public relations crowd feel they have to sell something positively. . . . We believe in being amateurish . . . but the public relations men want to put out four color brochures and dazzling artwork.

Businessmen who have been convinced of the utility of public relations in their own corporations have encouraged its application to help their favored civic and political causes. In fact, many of the public relations firms involved in politics began their political involvement at the request or sponsorship of one of their commercial clients and the majority reported having become involved in some campaigns through their commercial clients.

Herbert Baus, partner in a campaign management firm that was big in California during the 1950's and 1960's, began as a newspaperman, shifted to public relations and wound up in politics at the request of a group of businessmen. A reporter for the Washington *Post* in the early 1930's, Baus then went to work as a publicity man for the Junior Chamber of Commerce. During the Second World War he was a public relations man for the Air Corps.

After the war, he returned to public relations as the publicity director of the Los Angeles Chamber of Commerce and later set up his own public relations firm. The then president of the Los Angeles Chamber of Commerce asked Baus to manage the public referendum campaign against the proposition to establish a Fair Employment Practice Commission in California in 1946. He did, and it was defeated.

William Ross, the other partner in Baus and Ross, had always been interested in politics. He got his political ideals from his father, an elected town treasurer in Washington state, who held office until he was able to pay off the town's bonded debt. A fiscal conservative with strong views on what policy should be, Ross had no idea he could make a living at politics. He had a public relations firm in Los Angeles and drifted into politics because the owner of a mortuary he represented wanted his help in running for the Board of Education.

Baus and Ross were brought together in the late 1940's by some of their business clients. Ross had been managing public relations for the Los Angeles Home Show sponsored by the home building and banking industries. Baus had continued his connections with the Chamber of Commerce, even after he set up his own firm. When a proposition calling for the construction of low cost public housing in Los Angeles got onto the ballot, the home builders, banks and Chamber of Commerce asked Baus and Ross to join up to lead the campaign against the proposition. They did, and public housing was stopped.

Skeptical about being able to earn a living in political campaigns, Baus and Ross kept their commercial accounts even after they formed Baus and Ross Campaigns in 1948. During the 1950's, their commercial work began to decline in relation to their political work so they merged all their activities into Baus and Ross, Inc., in 1955. During the off-season, the company was stripped to the partners, a secretary and a bookkeeper. But during the campaign season, they expanded rapidly.

Through most of its busiest years, the company maintained close links with the business interests that had spawned it, managing ballot propositions and candidates that its business sponsors liked. In 1964, the firm managed the victorious Goldwater primary in California, but dropped out of participation in the general election campaign because the partners could not stomach the right-wingers who were running parts of the campaign. The same people returned to work for Reagan in 1966 and the firm of Baus and Ross found itself working for the Democratic candidate for governor for the first time.

In 1969, Baus retired from the campaign management business to write crossword puzzle books and dictionaries. His original business supporters called him back to battle in 1970, however, to run the campaign for a ballot proposition that would have allowed land companies and banks to operate more profitably in California. He spent $450,000 on the campaign but lost.

Advertising men have a route to political management that is similar to that of the public relations men, becoming involved in campaigns at the request of commercial clients. For most of the advertising men, political campaign management is a part-time thing; campaigns represent a small part of the total billings of advertising agencies.

One of the admen who sells both deodorants and candidates is Robert Goodman of Baltimore. However, he says they are different. Deodorants can be sold on name recognition alone, but candidates need to be loved as well. Spiro Agnew was his first political candidate. The basic media campaign was a song and scenes of Agnew surrounded by middle-aged ladies going ga-ga over him. Goodman liked those ads but thinks Agnew won because of opponent George ("Your home is your castle") Mahoney. The voters sent Mahoney back to his castle and they got Spiro Agnew, sex symbol.

Goodman likes the mix of commercial and political work but other admen have been bitten by the bug of politics and try to go into it full time. Treleaven, for example, quit as vice president and account manager of J. Walter Thompson to do political advertising. He handled the media portions of Bush's successful Texas campaign for the House of Representatives. After the campaign, he and Bush's campaign manager, James Allison, established a political consulting partnership, with Allison supervising the organizational aspects of a campaign and Treleaven the creative media portions. In 1968, Treleaven was the media director of the Nixon for President campaign.

When Nixon won, Allison became the deputy director of the Republican National Committee. His former partner signed on as a special consultant to the committee but stayed in the campaign consulting business, managing the media for several of the White House's target Senate seats in 1970. Early in 1971, the two re-formed their political consulting firm along with Ken Rietz, who had managed Brock's successful Senate campaign in Tennessee.

The 1968 Presidential campaign spawned shifts from commercial advertising to political advertising on the Democratic side as well. Allan Gardner was the account executive at Lennen and Newell in charge of the Humphrey account. He maintained his interest in politics after the campaign and brought it to his new firm of David Oksner and Mitchnik, where he headed a subsidiary devoted solely to political campaigns. Lennen and Newell also stayed in the political business. It established a subsidiary, Campaign Planners, Inc., to handle several major political campaigns in 1970. The subsidiary did research and campaign counseling in addition to the normal advertising services.

Journalism and public relations are still the most frequently-cited training grounds for professional managers, but people from television and radio are beginning to move into the field in increasing numbers. Almost all those who listed backgrounds in radio and television started their firms in the late 1960's. Roger Ailes, for example, first became involved in political campaigns during Nixon's 1968 campaign. Prior to that he was the producer of the Mike Douglas show, with no experience in politics. Now he heads a political consulting firm called REA Productions, which has offices in several cities. Ailes was heavily involved in helping to plan and carry out the media portions of several major political campaigns in 1970. In addition, he continued to serve as President Nixon's television advisor.

Robert D. Squier believes in television, and he is never very far away from it; a television set sometimes plays in the background as he sits working or talking in his office. He keeps a small videotape production unit ready for action in the next room. Squier, one of the new breed of managers who grew up on television, believes television makes the difference in modern campaigns. He started applying that belief all the way back in 1956, when he was a senior at the University of Minnesota and director of television for Orville Freeman's re-election campaign for governor. He laughs when he recalls that television was so unimportant then that they put "a kid" in charge of it. Now both Squier and television have grown up. To mark their maturity, Squier produced the first worldwide live telecast, "Our World," in 1967, winning an Emmy for his efforts.

Like many other managers, Squier dislikes working in the government, based on his two years during the Johnson Administration as director of television for U.S.I.A. He believed the United States could use television more effectively to present its position to people in other countries, but he quit in 1967 to return to National Educational Television because he found government administration "grim." Now he does what he likes—use television for something important.

Closely related to his belief in television's impact on people is Squier's conviction that what he himself does in a campaign makes a difference. He likes that feeling, too. He enjoys being in demand and having important and would-be important people come to him for help. Because he is in demand, and because he is convinced he makes a difference in the outcome, Squier works only for candidates he "digs." Sometimes he is brutally frank with the others who ask for his help.

In 1968, Squier wanted Humphrey to be President. He became director of television for the Democratic National Committee and television advisor to Humphrey. He was a member of the team that produced the Humphrey campaign and he was personally responsible for the election-eve telethon. Squier believes that program was a work of art that almost elected Humphrey. They tried to build a "debate" with Nixon, who was simultaneously appearing on another network. Squier left a chair and a used coffee cup on stage to make it look a bit amateurish and rushed to plant a few embarrassing questions to make sure it did not look phony. The only problem Squier had with Humphrey's telethon was Humphrey. The candidate arrived exhausted ten minutes before air-time because he insisted on stopping at one last union rally to see the crowd. An estimated 64 million people watched the telethon that night and if Neilsen determined the outcome of elections, Humphrey would be President. Squier won the telethon but Humphrey lost the election.

That did not shake Squier's belief in television one bit. He just thinks there was not enough of it in 1968. He argues that the Democrats had better candidates and better advertising and that once they got on the air, they started moving up rapidly in the polls. That is true, even if the cause and effect are not clear. The 1970 elections confirmed Squier's belief in the power of positive television. Those who had attempted to use television negatively, to scare people for example, had got in trouble; those who used it positively, to talk about real issues, had done very well.

Squier is interested in the quality, not the quantity, of political participation, aiming his television campaigns at the new "ticket-splitting" voter. That voter, he argues, is paying attention, seeking real information and discussion from television advertising. Squier is convinced that sloganeering and negativism just turn the ticket-splitters off. He does not really care about the rest of the voters, who are either committed unalterably to one party or less interested in politics. Those, he says, select themselves out of the election process. He does not think there is much point for his campaigns to deal with them, even though they are probably the majority of the electorate. For Squier, the individual who belongs to one party but who thinks about politics and splits his ticket to vote for a man he likes is the target. He wants that voter to love his candidate and uses polls to find out what message will make him do that.

With his belief that quality television and Bob Squier make a difference, he opened The Communications Company in early 1969. An initial non-political contract got him started. He worked in several 1969 races, including the Virginia gubernatorial primary and a mayoral race in Pennsylvania, and did preliminary planning and coaching for several potential 1970 candidates. Also in 1969, he and Napolitan teamed up again to run the re-election campaign of Ferdinand Marcos, President of the Philippines. Marcos became the first President of the Philippines to be re-elected; all the others who had tried had been defeated.

The following year, 1970, was a very good year for Bob Squier and The Communications Company. He was director of media or a television consultant in eight major races from Maine, where he worked for Muskie, to Hawaii, where he worked for Governor Burns's re-election. While he may be somewhat prejudiced, Squier is convinced that the 1970 nation-wide election-eve broadcast he produced for Muskie broke him out of the crowd of potential Democratic contenders for the Presidency. He is also convinced the Senator's talk helped win votes for Democrats all over the country the next day.

Squier and his company continued a close relationship with Muskie into 1972. Squier was retained on a part-time basis by the Muskie for President campaign in mid-1971. His contract called for full-time work for Muskie by the beginning of the 1972 primaries. The Communications Company moved into the same building as the Muskie campaign's first headquarters. While its own name was on the front door, a back door led from Squier's office to Muskie's. Squier believed that television would make Muskie President and himself a President-maker.

That close relationship remained as long as success seemed to be in the air, but once the cold winds of reality hit the Muskie campaign, Squier walked the plank. In the wake of Muskie's poor showing in the Florida and New Hampshire primaries in early 1972, controversy broke out in the Muskie camp. A number of his advisers were not satisfied with the radio and television spots that Squier produced and, conversely, Squier was unhappy with the material that was substituted. Squier resigned.

Second to communications as a training ground for professional managers is a traditional political party or staff position, with 11 percent of the managers coming from that kind of background. Most of them had been active as volunteers before they took staff positions. Their claim to power and influence in a campaign is more often based on their experience as organizers than as communicators. They tell candidate-clients that they have solved the organizational dilemmas posed by population growth and high mobility. In addition, they say they know where the candidates can get the communication skills they need.

Almost 75 percent of the firms owned by people with political backgrounds have been set up since 1965, with most of them relying almost completely on campaigns for their survival. The rapid expansion of this kind of campaign management firm is just another indication of the instability and lack of discipline in the political parties. As one of these managers admitted: "We should never have been allowed to develop. Everything I do should be done inside the political parties." The political parties, however, are almost powerless to stop the spread. The salaries that even prosperous party committees can afford to pay do not match what a successful manager can make on his own. In states where the party committees are bankrupt and have no control over primary battles, nothing can be done to stop party workers from setting up shop for themselves and working for wealthy individuals or interest groups that want to capture the party nominations.

The case of the Democrats in California after the 1966 Reagan victory is instructive. Many of the Democrats' professional campaign managers had been on the state government payroll and even those who worked directly for the party were dependent on contributions given because the party was in power. After the Republicans won, all of them became unemployed. That spurred the growth of several new professional campaign management firms.

Joseph Cerrell, for example, had been involved in Democratic Party politics for almost ten years. He quit graduate school to work for Brown in 1958, worked on the Kennedy campaign in 1960, was executive secretary of the party in the early 1960's, managed Salinger's 1964 campaign for the Senate and was finance director for Brown in 1966. He had always been a party organization employee but in 1967 the party was broke. He set up his own campaign management and lobbying business and by 1971 employed about 16 people, more than the Democratic party organization could dream of hiring.

Matt Reese talks with a West Virginia drawl and thinks with an IBM 360. If the 1964 election had not been a landslide, everyone in the country would have heard of him. As director of operations at the Democratic National Committee, he designed programs that registered more than two million new voters before the election. That probably would have been enough to elect any Democratic candidate, but, as it turned out, his two million new voters got lost in the rush to the polls to keep a "war-monger" out of the White House. After the 1964 election, Reese went home to West Virginia. He brought letters of high praise from the President but not fame. Only the professionals who had watched him work knew who he was. That turned out to be enough.

Reese had grown up in the poverty of West Virginia, with a burning ambition to gain economic security. While in school he got involved in politics by helping a professor run for Congress in 1954. He won, and Reese went off to Washington as his administrative assistant. He knew then that politics was a field in which he could find rapid success with little competition. The Washington honeymoon did not last long, however; Reese's boss lost his re-election campaign and they went back to West Virginia. Reese remained active in Democratic politics while earning a living as a salesman. He was executive secretary of the West Virginia Young Democrats when he met John F. Kennedy in 1959. He helped organize the West Virginia primary that was a key to Kennedy's plans and stayed on the campaign staff until the inauguration. He was given a job at the Small Business Administration, but he quickly moved to the Democratic National Committee.

When he returned home in 1965, there was a job for him in state government. But, like most managers, Reese did not like government administration. Besides, he had outgrown the confines of one state. He was restless, but he had no plans.

Some old friends from politics, who were running a primary to rid Kansas City of the remnants of the old Democratic machine, asked Reese to help them, at least on weekends. He did, and the Citizens for County Progress won 13 of the 14 primaries its candidates entered. Reese won, too. He found that he could do what he liked—work in Democratic campaigns—and make a living at the same time. As a result, Matt Reese Associates opened in October, 1966, with a contract from the Citizens for County Progress. The headquarters was in Washington, but for a while Reese maintained an office in Kansas City to service his original clients.

Reese sometimes claims that all he does is old-fashioned precinct organizing and campaigning with a few modern twists. He uses a computer to figure out which precincts will be most fruitful to work in. Then he uses telephone canvassers to recruit block captains in his priority precincts; they succeed in recruiting one worker for every nine calls they make. The block captains are his campaign workers. Another modern twist is that his precinct organization usually collapses the day the election is over. The volunteers have been recruited to do only one thing; when that is over, they have no further role.

Using Reese to recruit volunteers is expensive. He worries about the money he takes out of a campaign all the way to the bank. Reese believes that his overhead expenses (which are among the highest in the industry) make his services so expensive that he often prices himself out of the market. Nevertheless, he is busy. Between 1966 and 1970, Reese's firm worked in more than 25 different elections. In mid-1971, the firm was planning several statewide election contests for 1972 and had a contract to plan eight Presidential primaries for one of the Democratic contenders. In addition, the firm was working on communications and voters' rights programs for Common Cause, the new "citizens' lobby" in Washington. Even with all this activity, Reese may have trouble meeting his payroll because he is one of the few managers who tries to keep his professional staff of about ten on salary year round.

Reese fervently believes that everyone should be registered to vote. He also believes that if they were, the Democrats would never lose an election. The five shelves of donkeys that decorate Reese's office indicate that would be fine with him. In fact, when asked about Republicans, Reese responds, "I just don't like 'em."

Reese is happy doing "his thing" in politics but he feels he has to keep expanding and diversifying his services. Once he makes a full presentation on what he does or once he actually works in a campaign, the people he talked to or worked for often try to do it themselves. To stay ahead and to have something to sell the second time, he keeps adding new things. He is working with some pollsters to coordinate his own targeting systems with what they do. He also has set up a full campaign media planning and production service to give clients complete campaign planning. In 1971, he began doing political fund-raising for the first time.

Reese does not know how long it is all going to last, especially since campaigning with professionals is so expensive. However, he is enjoying it for the time being. If he thinks about the future too much he might get nervous. The firm in the country that is most like his, Spencer-Roberts of California, is in deep trouble after almost a decade of uninterrupted success in California.

Like Reese, Stu Spencer and Bill Roberts are methodical pluggers. They planned their campaigns carefully and kept tight control over them to make sure that the plans were followed. They were the shining national example of how to plan and manage Republican campaigns. But in 1970, when they should have had their finest and proudest year, things seemed to get out of control. They lost almost all of their major races and Republicans around the country started talking about Spencer-Roberts in the past tense.

The partners had always been skeptical about the future.

They knew that politicians want to know what you have done for them today. They were afraid that campaign management was a business you could get burned out in very easily; that they could be heroes one day and bums the next. Now they have some hard evidence. They went from nothing to the top and were on their way back down in ten years.

Spencer-Roberts is as strongly Republican as Matt Reese is Democratic. Other than that, there are few differences between them. The personal backgrounds and past experience in politics of the principals are about the same. Their feelings about their work are similar and they use the same assumptions about the electorate to plan their campaigns and even the same techniques.

Roberts was drawn into politics by Eisenhower's campaign for President. He likes to show visitors the library he is collecting of everything by and about Ike. He wanted to help the Eisenhower campaign in 1952 so he made contact with local Republican party leaders. They told him to go off and set up a Young Republican club. He did; in fact, it is still functioning.

He worked as a salesman for a living, but he found working his way up the Republican party hierarchy to be his real life. First he was active in the local Young Republican group he founded. Then he worked on the county level. Finally a chance came to do something full-time at the state level. John Rousselot (later a member of Congress and spokesman for the John Birch Society) was elected president of the California Young Republicans and brought Roberts in as executive director.

The Young Republicans were more interested in winning elections than in expounding right-wing philosophy in those days, so Roberts began working in election campaigns. He managed a special election for a seat in the state legislature in 1957. When the Alameda County Republican Committee started adding to its staff, Roberts signed on. From there, he was appointed executive director of the Los Angeles County Republican Committee. That was fine for about a year, but then a new county chairman was elected who wanted his own staff.

Spencer was a volunteer for Republican causes through most of the 1950's, too. He worked as the director of recreation for the city of Alhambra, California, but his own recreation was in Republican political campaigns. For him, politics was never work. In 1959, he joined Roberts on the staff of the Los Angeles County Republican Committee. Like Roberts, he was out of a job in a year.

Spencer really liked political campaigns. For him that was where the action was. As a behind-the-scenes manager, he could be near the fire, without really being in it. He thought being in the professional campaign management business was about the only way he could be satisfied in politics. He had worked in government and did not like it. He liked the election process, not the day-to-day operation of government. He and his partner also knew all too well that working for a political party was a very uncertain business. If they wanted to be in politics, it had to be through their own firm.

For almost ten years, they had watched their fellow Republicans pour money into professional campaign management firms. They believed they were as good as the "professionals" and thought they could get a piece of the action for themselves. Besides, they were both out of jobs. In 1960, they each put in $500, got three friends to hire them for campaigns and found themselves in the campaign management business. For their original clients, they relied on friends and politicians they had come to know during their years as Republican workers.

Spencer-Roberts skyrocketed to state and national attention in 1964 when they ran the Rockefeller for President primary in California. It was the big confrontation and the eyes of the nation and its journalists were focused on the strange politics of California. Rockefeller lost the primary in California, but Spencer-Roberts won. Every politician in the state knew who they were and what they could do.

Even one of Goldwater's principal supporters knew that

Roberts and Spencer were the people to see in California about campaigning as a Republican. Reagan approached them in 1965 and, after their success in putting him in the governor's chair, their political wizardry was in great demand. Not satisfied with winning the governorship, the Republicans set their eyes on the state legislature, still controlled by the Democrats.

The state Republican Party, under the leadership of Harry Parkinson, mapped a long-term plan to get control of the legislature by the time the 1970 reapportionment came around. Naturally, they called in Spencer-Roberts to do the work. Under the Calplan, Spencer-Roberts were busy throughout the year planning state legislative races. Through massive efforts by Spencer-Roberts in special elections, the Republicans got control of the state legislature by 1969, one year ahead of schedule. They lost control again in 1970.

Throughout the 1960's, Spencer-Roberts had tried to keep one step ahead of the competition. They were alone at the top of the Republican Party but they always acted as if someone was breathing down their neck about to take over the lead. In 1966, they set up an electronic data processing subsidiary to do basic research on voting behavior and to do computer analysis of election districts. Vince Barabba, a young statistician who had worked as a field organizer in the Rockefeller primary, was brought in to be president of Datamatics. The work of Spencer-Roberts and their subsidiary with the Republican Congressional Committee and with the American Medical Political Action Committee kept the firm far ahead of the other Republican management firms.

The subsidiary was reorganized in 1969 to account for its acquisition of a political polling capability. Dick Wirthlin, a highly-respected Republican pollster from Arizona, joined the firm, which was reorganized as Decision Making Information. DMI remained a subsidiary but it went out on its own to solicit polling and computer work from Republican campaigns outside California. By 1970, it wanted to do its own campaign consulting, too. The firm also started soliciting non-political commercial computer work.

At the beginning of the 1970 campaign season, everything looked rosy for Spencer-Roberts. They had major contracts for the gubernatorial and state legislative races in California. Spencer himself was to manage five state legislative races. In addition, the firm had management or counseling contracts in seven election contests outside California, from Michigan and Alabama to Hawaii. By the time the election came, the partners probably wished they had never been so successful.

Reagan won again, but this time it was no victory for Spencer-Roberts. Disputes between the governor's staff and the campaign managers resulted in Roberts' early departure from the scene to work for George Murphy's Senatorial re-election campaign. Murphy lost badly. Spencer-Roberts did not fare well in the state legislative races, either, as the Democrats regained control of the State Assembly. Outside the state, Spencer-Roberts candidates lost, too. The Republican losses could not be really blamed on the professional managers, but the firm had taken a good part of the credit when Republicans won and they were given a good part of the blame when they lost.

The problems for Spencer-Roberts did not end on Election Day. Their contract with the state Republican Committee for continuing consulting and work on state legislative elections was not renewed. Spencer was to be hired on a per diem basis by the state committee as needed. Moreover, by early 1971, simmering difficulties between Spencer-Roberts and its subsidiary, Decision Making Information, broke into the open and the two firms separated with some bitterness.

Perhaps Spencer-Roberts had seen more about the professional campaign management industry looking down at everyone else from the top than was appreciated by others. It had been pessimistic about the future while everyone else in the business was holding it up as the model. In late 1971, the firm was still very much in business and it would probably have enough work in the 1972 elections to keep it busy. But something had changed. Spencer and Roberts were no longer the people to see in California about Republican campaigns.

While formal research and public opinion polling are major parts of the modern professionally-managed campaign, the universities of the country have not made much impact or contribution to the campaign management industry. About 10 percent of the firms in the survey called themselves public opinion or behavioral research companies, but only 3 percent of the people who participated in the study had formal training in this area. Many pollsters are apparently doing business on self-taught skills.

Hal Evry, one of the most colorful and outspoken campaign managers, got into the business from behavioral research. He established the Western Opinion Research Center in 1946 to do private polling and market research. He believes that good polling, advertising and campaign management can elect anyone who has an IQ of more than 120. Evry is so confident of his techniques and contemptuous of the traditional political process that he discourages his candidates from making public appearances during a campaign. Whenever a candidate makes a speech, he argues, somebody gets mad or asks a question the candidate can't answer. To avoid these possible pitfalls, Evry likes to hide his candidates behind mass media advertising over which he has complete control. The candidate gets his message across to the great bulk of the electorate without subjecting himself to either the voters or "95-dollar-a-week reporters who don't know anything about politics."

Among the pro's, Evry is not well liked. Many of the other managers dismiss him as a sham and charlatan and are annoyed by his tactics of running ads to recruit candidates for his paying clients and writing about what he does in places like *Life* Magazine. Evry himself shakes off the criticism by arguing that he is just more open and honest than the others are about the farce that now passes for democratic elections. He may be right because one of the most "respected" managers in the professional campaign business has about the same approach to campaigns as he does.

Joe Napolitan fervently believes in polls, controlled and positive television communication and professional campaign management. He believes everybody in electoral politics should use them: the Democrats, the Republicans, the parties in the Philippines, Britain, France, Belgium, everybody. He is constantly jetting around the world to practice and promulgate his art. Like a messenger from the future, Napolitan arrives on the wings of a big bird, tells the politicians to take polls—and follow them—and communicate through the electronic media; then he gets on the bird again to deliver his message in another place, perhaps halfway around the world. Napolitan seems to revel in far-flung campaigning as if his travel schedule itself is his principal marketing device. A man whose presence is required in New York, Washington, London, Madrid, and Manila in the next three weeks must be a truly important and talented person. So, when Mike Gravel called from Alaska in November 1966 to set up an appointment to talk about planning his 1968 race for the U.S. Senate, he was told that while Napolitan would be in Tripoli, Rome, Milan, Paris and London for the next three weeks, he would stop by in Anchorage on his way home from London to Springfield, Massachusetts.

The delay was well worth Gravel's time, for Napolitan planned a two-year successful effort to capture the U.S. Senate seat held by Alaska's patriarch Ernest Gruening that is still viewed as the classic example of the new politics of polling and mass media. Napolitan told Gravel to take polls to determine what was needed to beat Gruening in the primary, play a visible but non-political role for more than a year to build up public recognition without appearing to be a threat to Gruening, and then beat Gruening with a television blitz of the best materials ever produced and shown in Alaska. Considering there would be about 35,000 voters in the primary and 80,000 in the general election, a prodigious effort was undertaken. Several polls were taken to assess Gravel's and Gruening's strengths and weaknesses. Not too surprisingly, Gruening's age—82—was the principal strike against him. Napolitan set out to make Gravel an acceptable and respectable alternative to the old man.

The campaign spawned its own monthly magazine called *Alaska Today*, which was distributed as a Sunday supplement with all the newspapers in the state. The magazine was ostensibly non-partisan; it just happened to have regular feature and cover stories about Mike Gravel. The magazine touted Gravel as a great Speaker of the Alaska House of Representatives and as a great land-developer for Alaska's future. It was all very soft sell.

Gravel trailed Gruening in the polls for the whole year before the primary, but ten days before the election, Napolitan unveiled his secret weapon: a thiry-minute biographic film shown simultaneously on all Alaskan television stations and then repeated many times on each station before the election. The polls turned around virtually overnight and Gravel kept his lead, winning the primary and the general election even though Gruening decided to wage a write-in campaign. Both Napolitan and Gravel argue that polls and television made the difference in Alaska in 1968, but the same formula used the next year lost when it was applied to the gubernatorial campaign of Larry Carr.

Napolitan does not believe in issues or political parties, and they are not very important in the campaigns he runs. In fact his definition of the new politics is "communicating a candidate's message directly to the voter without filtering it through the party organization." Modern campaigns, he argues, are won and lost within the confines of the planner's desk, not in the wards. How the planner reads the polls and what he puts on the television which he buys and controls are the keys to success. For Napolitan, issues are merely a vehicle for communicating some emotional image, or sparking a campaign organization. Napolitan's favorite devices include thirty-minute emotional biographies broadcast on television along with short spots and big direct mail promotions. Napolitan and most other professional managers prefer television because they can keep doing scenes over until the candidate gets it right, or they can edit the material to their liking.

During the 1968 campaign, Napolitan urged Hubert Humphrey to make a dramatic break on Vietnam with President Johnson as a bold step needed to get the campaign out of the doldrums. The question of Humphrey's (or even Napolitan's) own beliefs about Vietnam were not relevant to this policy recommendation. The campaign needed a dramatic breakthrough to show that Humphrey was an independent leader. The Vietnam issue seemed to be a good vehicle, but it might just as easily have been something else.

Humphrey lost the 1968 election, but Napolitan didn't. He looked like a hero who almost pulled the whole mass together, and since Joe McGinniss has not been allowed to look over his shoulder no one would have to know that there was no real difference. Napolitan became the man to see in Democratic campaigning. People like Nordy Hoffman, the executive director of the Democratic Senatorial campaign committee, urged incumbents up for re-election in 1970 to sit down with Napolitan to talk about their campaigns and even the Luddite-dominated AFL-CIO COPE used Napolitan's counsel for the 1970 campaigns. Other professionals like Bob Squier said they just got the scraps that fell off Napolitan's table.

To make sure no one missed the rise of the professional manager to the top of American politics, Napolitan set about creating the International and American Associations of Political Consultants almost immediately after the campaign was over. The International Association was formed in late 1968 in Paris under Napolitan's guidance and the American Association held its first meeting in New York in January, 1969. The International Association holds annual meetings in different European cities and gives its members (largely Americans who manage campaigns and corporate/government relations) an opportunity to exchange notes and hobnob with local political figures. The 1970 meeting was held in London to spur interest in the group among British politicians. Instead, the meeting was virtually boycotted by the British and roasted in the British press for being an attempt to commercialize politics. Other meetings in Paris, Florence and Brussels have been more successful.

The American Association has two or three seminars a year for professional managers, and now publishes a quarterly magazine on professional campaign management, *Politeia*. Napolitan has been the moving force in both groups. In 1972 he was president of the International Association and past president of the American group. The presidency of the American Association was passed on to Napolitan's close friend and business partner, F. Clifton White. While Napolitan works only for Democrats and White works only for conservative Republicans, the two see eye to eye on most other things. In the old politics of partisanship, Republicans and Democrats usually traveled in different circles. In the new politics of professional management, the election men stick close to their own party in elections but then laugh it off with their professional and business colleagues from the other party after the campaign is over.

One of the people who moved most successfully from the academic world into the campaign management industry is F. Clifton White, considered by many politicians one of the shrewdest political managers in the business. White began his career in politics after World War II while he was teaching political science at Cornell when some friends convinced him he would make a great Congressman. He ran in the primary and lost. In the process, he learned how little he knew about politics, and vowed to learn all about it. He found few books that were worth much, so he decided to learn by doing. White learned about politics by moving through the chairs of local, state and national party office. He was a precinct worker, ward leader and then city chairman of the Republican Party in Ithaca, New York. He studied each job from the inside out and developed job descriptions for each. While he was city chairman in Ithaca, he managed a successful mayoral race. Electing a mayor of Ithaca, a city of fewer than 7,000 voters, may not be much, but it was White's first success. Like many of the professional managers, White recalls his first taste of political victory as his most exciting.

White set out from Ithaca to teach the world about American electoral politics. Operating from a simple office in New York, adorned only by framed copies of the Constitution and the Declaration of Independence, he teaches politics to a large and important student body. He gives seminars on practical politics to businessmen, teaches Republican candidates he likes about winning on the right, teaches and learns from other professional managers and tells the corporations and governments who can pay his fees all about the current and future political climate.

White's firm, F. Clifton White Associates, was not set up as a campaign management firm; its principal business is training programs in practical politics for corporations and trade associations, one of the first organized to teach businessmen how to be active and successful in electoral politics. The courses are formally bi-partisan although most of the business executives are Republicans. Before he was such a well-identified political figure, White kept his students in the dark about his own political leanings by telling nasty stories about both parties.

In the early days, White went around the country conducting seminars for company executives at different locations. Now he tries to develop programs that can be fit into the regular training program of a corporation. He trains the permanent training officers of the company to teach the local managers how to be effective in politics. The whole idea of corporate-based political education is a boon to businesses. What better way could there be for a company to develop a favorable political climate than to have its own employees in charge of the local party organizations and public offices?

The teacher in White also comes out in the campaigns he decides to run. He managed the Goldwater campaign for the Republican nomination in 1964 (but not the general election campaign), the Reagan campaign for the Republican nomination in 1968 and the Buckley for Senate campaign in New York in 1970. In each of these campaigns, he wanted to teach the Republican Party and the nation that the political action ought to be on the right. White firmly believes that the moderate and conservative elements of the population can be united into a majority coalition that is led by conservatives. He manages political campaigns for friends and associates when he thinks he can make his point.

Almost immediately after the Buckley campaign in 1970, White turned to another of his teaching activities. The American Association of Political Consultants held a seminar in November, 1970, for all the professionals to get together to tell each other "how we did it." He helped set up the professional managers association to foster exchange of information among the professionals themselves and between the professionals and the academic community. White believes it is possible for all the competitors in the field to get together and talk about what they do because he thinks there are few "secrets" in managing political campaigns. For him, campaigns are just the effective utilization of scarce resources and management techniques. If all the campaigns used their resources well, he argues, the voters would be presented with a clearer picture of their candidates and a better choice. That, he concludes, is what democracy is all about.

White thinks this is true for all "free world" countries. He was also one of the founders of the International Association of Political Consultants. The association, largely

American and Western European, meets annually to discuss developments in campaign techniques and to review what happened in elections during the year. While the impetus for setting up the association was largely American, White does not see it as a new and subtle tool for American political intervention in the affairs of other countries. Rather, he sees the association as a way to respond to the tremendous interest he has found throughout the world in American electoral techniques. He also thinks Americans have something to learn from European techniques.

In recent years, White has been doing another kind of political education, governmental affairs advising. As both government and business have grown to monstrous size, their fortunes have become intertwined. Present and future government policy is one of the major determinants of whether or not a given business investment decision will be possible or profitable. Corporations need more than a ouija board to guess about what the future political climate will be and so they hire governmental affairs advisors to help them find out. White believes that his broad experience as a political operative all over the country and as a successful manager of electoral politics makes him eminently qualified to interpret the political climate for clients. He and several other people with similar experience have established a company called Public Affairs Analysts.

F. Clifton White, leading Republican campaign manager; Joseph Napolitan and Michael Rowan, Democratic campaign managers; Martin Ryan Haley, a corporate/governmental affairs advisor in the United States and Europe; and Nicholas Constantine, an international corporate lawyer, are business partners. Associated with them are several leading European and American politicians and governmental affairs advisors. Public Affairs Analysts has offices or answering services in ten major European and American cities and correspondents in all 50 states and all continents of the world.

The introductory brochure for the company lists 40 different kinds of analysis, counseling and services available to corporate and institutional clients around the world, all of them dealing with the relations between business and government or politics. They range from a complete analysis of a corporation's government relations needs, capabilities and objectives to speech writing for corporate officials. In between, the firm offers such things as lobbying programs designed for any corporate objective before any governmental body in the world and "evaluation of political movements, parties and candidates at all levels, domestic and international." The firm says it will provide any political, public affairs or governmental relations services except political campaign management within the United States. That limitation apparently is designed to eliminate possible conflicts of interest among the bi-partisan partners. Clients include American and multinational corporations and governments interested in political developments in other countries.

The partnership is a curious arrangement. The principals are divided on who shall govern in the United States, but united in offering political "fix-it" services to corporate clients who can pay the fee. A voter might well ask what difference voting for a Democrat or a Republican makes if the managers will just get together after the election to advise corporations how to get what they want no matter who wins. The partners, of course, do not see any such conflict.

The movement from managing mayoral campaigns in Springfield and Ithaca to a global political action company represents a phenomenal pyramiding of private political power. If Public Affairs Analysts is for real (it may after all just be a front for U.S. interference in other countries' politics) the partners have constructed a world-wide political organization that can serve world-wide corporate interests. National boundaries and voters have no real meaning in this game. The existence of such a firm and the partnership in it of leading Republicans and Democrats leads to the question of what it is that the professional campaign managers are after.

CHAPTER 6

Amateurs
and Professionals

Few experiences I know, save perhaps having an orgasm, equal the feeling on election night when the vote reports start coming in and it looks as though you are going to spring an upset.
—*Joe Napolitan.*

Politics is where the action is. It's the main tent. There are other power elites, society, the military, business, but they are all side shows.
—*Max Berking, New York advertising man /and Westchester County Democratic Chairman*

At the national committee, the money people still controlled things. I had to go over my plans with ignoramuses.
—*A Washington-based consultant.*

I don't consider myself a political hack. I think I can walk away from it. . . . If I don't believe in a guy I don't have to work for him. . . . I like the independence, coming in contact with people, and the wheeling and dealing.
—*Joe Cerrell.*

The motivations and goals of the professional campaign managers need to be clearly defined if their impact on American politics is to be understood. Their personal goals form screens that color everything they see and touch in politics, play a major part in the shape of the companies the professionals establish for their activities and affect the ways in which the managers view their work and the electorate. Further, the goals and motivations of the professional managers help determine both what they do and the methods they employ. The managers may not be able to get what they want; some of the goals may be ambiguous or inconsistent and other factors may intervene. However, as the professional campaign managers become more central to the electoral process, we shall all be unwilling participants in their struggle.

The people who own campaign management companies are professional politicians in the most precise meaning of that term. Additionally, however, they view themselves as technical professionals with an expertise that should bring them recognition, personal independence and security. Despite their diversity in background and training, there is almost complete uniformity in the reasons managers give for establishing their own firms. They have set up campaign management firms so they can simultaneously engage in politics, make lots of money and gain professional respect and independence. It is almost as if the professional managers, like other groups, are demanding their "liberation."

James Q. Wilson has described a professional politician as a person who is principally concerned with the outcome of politics—winning or losing—nothing else. For the professional, there is something special about participation itself, about being in on the action. The status rewards of playing the game of politics are very important for the professional politician. Wilson differentiated the professional from the amateur, who is more motivated by ideas and principles than by the game itself. For the amateur, politics is only a means to achieve public policy aims; it is not satisfying by itself.

The vast majority of the participants in this study demonstrate the motivations Wilson attributed to the professional politicians. The more a person is involved in campaign management, the closer he is likely to resemble Wilson's definition of a professional politician. Several of the questions included in both the oral interviews and mail questionnaires used in this study were designed to probe why the managers become involved in political campaigns. The characteristics Wilson used to describe professionals came through strongly in the answers supplied by the managers. Of those most heavily involved in campaigning, 72 percent said they "like the feeling of winning," 76 percent responded that "politics is where the action is," 80 percent checked, "We make good money in political campaigns," 50 percent said, "We have a civic responsibility to use our skills for the public good," and 44 percent said the idea of a civic responsibility to use their skills for public good was not very important at all.

The responses were quite different from those whose firms were less heavily involved in political campaigns. They retained some of the characteristics of amateurs—59 percent said "politics is where the action is," 45 percent said they "make good money in political campaigns" and 71 percent responded, "We have a civic responsibility to use our skills for the public good." Only 25 percent of the less heavily involved managers dismissed the idea of a civic responsibility as not important.

When one of the managers was asked why he was in the business, he responded for most of his colleagues by saying, "Winning; it's all a big crapshoot." It is normal for people who play a game to want to win, but not everybody has the same drive or need to win. Many of the managers moved into political campaigning from fields in which winning and losing were less well defined. For the majority of the managers, the possibility of winning in such a clearly visible way was what made political campaigning so attractive; 60 percent said it was important to them that they could see the result of their work on Election Day. One of the most successful managers said:

> In most public relations work you never know for sure how you are doing. Here, it's like a war or a game. You have a grid and you play it to a conclusion. I like the combat, the warfare of ideas. Public relations is ephemeral. In politics you can score.

In their need to win, the managers are like other and more traditional professional politicians. One of the things that makes them different is the steps they have taken to insulate themselves against the risk of losing. Winning is the important goal, but the firm can absorb some losses without any great catastrophe. Most of the professional management firms work for several candidates in different places at the same time. They want to win them all, but they know that if some of their candidates lose they will still come out all right. It's like playing with a slightly loaded deck of cards; the odds of winning are more heavily in your favor but there is still some risk, and you still have the crisp measurement of Election Day.

This is not to say that losing is good for business. Most managers know that losing is very bad both for their egos and for their businesses. However, working on several elections at the same time helps cushion the damage from losing. In the 1970 elections, the trend was toward the Democrats so the major Republican firms had a particularly bad year. They were involved in some spectacular losses, as well as some less-noticed victories. One of the Republican firms that was prominent in several major losing races was Bailey, Deardourff and Bowen, which worked for Raymond J. Broderick against Milton Shapp for governor in Pennsylvania, Roger Cloud against John Gilligan for governor in Ohio, and for Nelson Gross against Harrison Williams for the Senate in New Jersey, all of whom lost. The firm may or may not have contributed to these defeats. It is possible that the candidates would have lost by even more votes if the firm had not been there. However, the reality was that the candidates lost and Bailey, Deardourff and Bowen was there, high on the list of those who are said to have had a bad year in 1970. That may not really affect the firm's future, however, because it also had some winners. To overcome its own record problems, the company published a little brochure entitled "How Bailey, Deardourff and Bowen Helped Us Win." It featured seven of its successful candidates from the 1968, 1969 and

1970 elections, including Senator Schweiker of Pennsylvania, Senator Saxbe of Ohio, Representatives DuPont of Delaware and Kemp of New York, and Governors Cahill of New Jersey and Milliken of Michigan. Bailey, Deardourff and Bowen may or may not have had any impact on the outcome of these winning elections either, but it wanted politicians, party officials and potential candidate-clients to know it had been there, too.

While losing too much may damage future business prospects, the need to win that is felt by professional managers goes well beyond economics. It is a measurable sign of achievement; it is the way campaign managers prove their worth as men and professionals. Most of the other major actors in electoral politics do not rely on the campaign itself to win the respect and support of their colleagues. Candidates depend more on what they do in office or in private life to win the respect of their fellow politicians. They have two, four or six years to show what they can do. For many of them, the campaign is an unpleasant interlude. For the manager, the campaign is it. He has to succeed on Election Day.

The most satisfying victory for a manager is to win against the odds. They know they must have winners to stay in business, but they do not concentrate on clients who would be sure winners without them, first, because most sure winners know enough not to throw money away on a management firm and, second, because there isn't enough challenge. For a campaign to be satisfying, managers need to believe that their presence and skills make a big difference in the outcome. While most of the managers interviewed said they wanted candidate-clients who could win, they did not list the probability that a candidate would win as an important criterion in their decision to work for him. Several of the managers said flatly that they did not like getting involved in sure things, but were more interested in marginal races where their help would make the difference. Others said they looked for a few sure winners each year to keep the total win-lose record high and therefore give them some leeway in taking more marginal but interesting campaigns.

There is a real tension, visible in almost all the professional managers, between the commercial need to have a good win-lose record and the personal need to win in a challenging situation. The remarks of two managers are representative:

> We are not interested in taking acknowledged winners. We want people who are close but who might lose without us. Our candidates are usually rated 40–49 percent in the polls.

> I should demand a poll before I take a candidate to see if he is in the ball game. But I like these guys. I want them to win . . . The record of wins ought to be related to [the number of] candidates who had a chance.

Making good money in political campaigns is important to the professional managers for the same reason. Money feeds both their families and their need to have their success measured in terms everyone can see. The size of the fees managers get often reflects their status in the industry.

The professional managers can make much more money running campaigns than they can legally in any other part of politics. This is especially true if the managers are collecting the 15 percent advertising commission paid to agencies on all mass media advertising. In some cases, the professional managers make more money running a campaign than the candidate will make in his whole term of office. For the time being at least, campaign management has become the place to make money in politics. Legal limitations on television and radio advertising may cut into the profitability of some firms, but most of the activities of managers will probably be unchecked by legal reforms. In fact, the managers may become more valuable as they advise candidates how to make the best possible use of legally limited communication resources.

By establishing firms that work only in elections, the professionals can participate in the part of politics they enjoy, elections, and avoid any responsibility for the part of politics they dislike, government policy-making and administration. Almost none of the managers interviewed said they would accept a governmental job. Most were rather blunt in their distaste for governmental work. As one of them said: "I like campaigns . . . But I have no interest in government at all. I would never take a government position."

Governmental work, especially in the bureaucracy, has none of the things that attract the managers to politics. It is slow and continuous and it is much harder to measure success. Even the day-to-day problems of elected office would be frustrating to most of the managers. In addition, the managers know that while power flows around government, it is not limited to the people with formal positions. If they want political power for themselves, they can get it outside government. Besides, they can make much more money outside the government than in it.

The professional managers believe their firms can help them achieve other goals that would not have been realistic if they stayed with traditional political organizations. More than 80 percent of all the participants in this study are convinced they are bringing important technological innovations to politics and that they are providing professional services that politicians need.

The most unanimous finding in this entire study revolves around the managers' self-image of professionalism. More than anything else, the people who have established campaign management firms believe they are skilled professional researchers, communicators and organizers. They argue strongly that they bring scientific, or at least objective, views into an arena long dominated by myth and incompetence. One of the most frequently-voiced complaints from the professional managers is about the dolts and dullards they are forced to work with in campaigns. Sometimes these complaints are against candidates, but more often they are against the people in the political parties who have traditionally run electoral campaigns. The professional managers separate themselves from other actors in politics on the basis of their technical skills.

The simple table below shows clearly that campaigns can be managed by people who have different mixes of motivations and skills.

In fact, all these combinations can be seen operating side by side in our political system. Some of the lesser-involved firms that participated in this study are run by men with professional skills and amateur motivations. They spend most of their time using their skills in regular commercial business and work in campaigns only occasionally. As one of them put it, "When things get bad, I get in." Many traditional party leaders have professional motivations but no technical communications skills, and volunteers in campaigns often have both amateur motivations and amateur skills. Several hundred of this last type serve as volunteer campaign managers for Congressional candidates every two years and almost always lose.

While traditional forms of participation and political or-

Types of People Who Work in Campaigns

SKILLS	ATTITUDES	
	Professional attitudes	Amateur attitudes
Technical Skills	Professional managers	Less-involved professional managers
Amateur Skills	Party leaders and cadre	Volunteer campaign workers

ganization might satisfy a manager's desire for action, they could not fulfill in any way his desire for recognition as a professional with special skills. As a member of an elected official's or candidate's staff, an individual remains submerged under the personality and presence of the public figure, no matter what his own professional skills are. Personal political staffs in the United States are traditionally invisible and the political advisors whose names are recognized are the exception rather than the rule, although this is beginning to change as the media cover behind-the-scenes maneuvers better.

The professional managers have lost the traditional advisor's "passion for anonymity" because of their self-perception as skilled professionals. It is probably too much to ask a politician to remain quietly in the background when he thinks he is bringing important technological innovations to American politics, making up for weaknesses in the political system, and winning elections for people who would otherwise lose. Why should such a person let his reputation rise or fall with a political candidate or party official who may not even be following his advice? Why shouldn't he demand and get recognition on his own? The private firm allows him to try to do just that.

As one of the managers said, "If we wanted to stay in politics, it came down to doing this." People with professional skills and needs see owning their own campaign management firms as an opportunity to succeed in both the traditional and modern sense. They can have all the action and challenge of electoral politics without any of the responsibility of government and still gain recognition from their peers and the attentive public for their individual skills. For them, the professional campaign management firm is an opportunity to achieve the goal of most politicians, an independent and recognized position of strength in the political system that is somewhat secure from the vagaries and uncertainties of party and electoral politics. After some time, the firm may not give the managers the security and recognition they seek, but in the rough and tumble worlds of politics, advertising and public relations, the temptation to try is very strong.

The professional managers think their firms give them independence in several different ways. They feel they have more leeway in picking the people for whom they will work and an alternative to stay out of a campaign if they don't like any of the candidates. Only 19 percent of the firms that participated said they were usually hired as the result of active solicitation of campaign work; rather, the most frequent procedure is for the candidate or his campaign committee to contact the firm. This is especially true for the most well-known firms. Others, in the words of one manager, "solicit like hell." A few even pay a "finder's fee" to go-betweens who introduce them to clients.

The managers also feel the firm gives them an institutional framework in which they can be solicited or from which they can look for business discreetly. Almost all the managers interviewed said they got many more job offers than they could accept in a year.

When hired by a candidate, the professional consultant can set some of the ground rules. About 70 percent of the participating managers, for example, said that the candidate must be willing to do what they tell him to and be able to pay promptly for the kind of campaign they think he should run. Few people being hired for staff positions can get that kind of agreement.

The kind of independence professional managers perceive they have in their firms can be seen in their attitude toward the post-election period. They want to end their relationship on Election Day. One of the media managers could not even recall the name of one of his major 1970 clients seven months after the election. Of the 50 firms that were most heavily involved in political campaigns, 96 percent said that what the candidate might do for them and their other clients after he was elected was not important at all as a criterion for deciding who to work for. That is a remarkable change from the traditional orientation of a professional politician.

In interviews, the managers placed heavy stress on their independence. One said:

> It's a great business. You tell people exactly what you think and they pay you . . . If we don't like a guy we tell him we don't want to have anything to do with him.

Another said he preferred going into a campaign as a volunteer (his fee being paid by an outside supporter of the candidate) because he could "lose patience with the people who didn't know what was going on" and move freely to do what he thought was necessary.

In addition to being more or less free to choose who he will work for, the professional manager feels he is independent of the fate of one political leader. The traditional staff of a professional politician rises and falls with one leader or group. Some individual staff members have been able to survive in politics, even if the particular person or clique they worked for loses, but the process is uncertain and often involves starting from scratch several times with new bosses in new places. The modern professional tries to avoid this. He works simultaneously with several different groups, probably in different geographic areas, to reduce the possibility of disaster and increase the probability of some success.

Being involved in several elections simultaneously helps professional managers achieve professional recognition, too. Working on the staff of an individual politician or of a party, their skills might go unnoticed. Participation in several campaigns, however, gives a firm more opportunities to promote its own professional talents in addition to advancing the causes of its clients.

In a single campaign it would be difficult to attribute success or failure to one person. However, if a campaign consultant is simultaneously involved in several campaigns he can promote his own contribution to those races with more ease.

It is precisely this independence that some elected political leaders and party officials resent. They believe that having their staff's futures depend upon their own success helps insure loyalty and top-notch work. The Kennedys, for example, have always been nervous about people in their campaigns who were "in business for themselves" rather than for the candidate.

Campaign organizations collapse within hours after the polls close. Traditionally, even full-time campaign managers often had no idea what they would do after the campaign was over. The professional with his own firm is spared that uncertainty. When the elections are over, he will have his company and his office. In fact, this security may be false. He may have no business waiting and few prospects, but the myth of security and independence may be as important as the reality.

Running just below the surface of the professional manager's desire for independence may be a desire for his own political power base. Some managers eschew personal political power. Others trade on their access to politicians on a grand scale as lobbyists or governmental affairs representatives. Whatever his purpose, the firm is a political asset the professional manager controls.

In summary, the people who run professional campaign management firms are professional politicians who have set up companies to enjoy the action of politics, get rich, gain political and organizational independence and to bask in the warm light of professional recognition and respect.

The campaign managers have gone a long way toward meeting their goal of professional recognition. Their visibility and the common awareness it brings are the first important steps toward professional organization. As long as campaign managers remained individual members of a political staff, tucked in some nondescript corner, the basis of professional organization and recognition did not exist. The emergence of firms has changed all that and helped lead the managers toward the recognition and respect they think they deserve.

Not all occupations are professions. The notion of a profession suggests that there are bonds beyond a similarity in work. Members of a profession have a strong group consciousness not shared by outsiders. It is precisely this consciousness that campaign managers have been seeking.

Social scientists have suggested five criteria for measuring the degree to which an occupation has turned into a profession. First, the group must operate on a basis of a commonly understood and accepted systematic theory; the theoretical base of a professional group may be subject to continuing dispute and change and it may be more or less formal, but it must exist. Second, the professional's authority must be recognized by the clientele. Third, this authority must have broad community sanction. Fourth, the professionals themselves need to develop their own culture, usually through professional associations. Finally, the practitioners must be guided by a code of ethics in their relations with their clients and colleagues. The code, too, may be more or less formal, as, for example, the canons of ethics for lawyers and the Hippocratic Oath and general ethics of practice for doctors.

While they are not easily measured, these criteria at least provide a way of judging how far along the road to professionalism the campaign managers have traveled. One observer, Dan Nimmo, believes the managers have acquired the trappings of a profession without much of the substance. Most of the managers themselves believe the substance has been there for some time and that the trappings are just now being added. The reality is somewhere in between.

Nimmo's criticism is based on his belief that the managers have no operational theory. He argues that the managers rarely analyze the problems of their clients systematically, and that for the most part, they operate on a trial and error basis. The theoretical base upon which managers plan and run campaigns may not be well stated, or even completely accurate, but it does exist. While there are measurable and important differences in personal political ideology between managers who are Democrats and those who are Republicans, there is no discernible difference in the ways they approach their work. The great majority of the managers have the same perceptions about the roles they play in campaigns, and about the things that are important to them. Additionally, the managerial techniques they use and the assumptions they make about voters are remarkably similar.

The theoretical base of the campaign management profession draws heavily on several other professions. However, the amalgam is creating a new body of theory about human organization and behavior. The managers draw from organization theory and from voting behavior theory most heavily. As one leading manager said: "There are no secrets in managing a campaign. The management principles are all the same." Thus, he argued, managers could exchange ideas and experiences freely and usefully.

A substantial number of managers from both parties made written campaign organization and strategy plans available for examination in this study. The similarities were remarkable. Republican and Democratic managers have a nearly common image of the ideal campaign organization, and the internal campaign organizations they recommend to candidates are very similar. Perhaps they have arrived at this common view more from experience than from formal analysis. The result, however, is the same. The more managers write and talk about their campaigns, the more formalized their organizing principles will become. The professional campaign management industry is becoming a center of experimentation and theory building in the areas of temporary organization, mass media research and communication and political behavior.

The campaign managers apply a nearly uniform set of assumptions about voter behavior to the campaigns they plan, drawn both from their own experience and from formal social science research done by academics and campaign managers over the past 25 years. Some of the conclusions managers have drawn about the voters may be wrong. The important thing, however, is the uniformity with which these ideas are held within the industry and the frequency of their use. By these measures, the campaign managers have and use enough theory to justify their claim of professionalism.

Campaign managers have clearly achieved the second criterion of professionalism, recognition from their clientele. This can be seen in the rapid growth of the industry and in the comments made by politicians about the campaign managers. Even the elected politicians who are most critical of the managers and their techniques admit they had arrived to stay. One politician said that professional campaign managers were the worst thing that ever happened to politics, but that he would probably be forced to use them in his next campaign because he could not get the talent he needed elsewhere.

The conspicuous losses of managers in the 1970 campaigns may have produced some new skepticism and caution, but that has not interfered with the acceptance of the presence of a professional manager in a campaign. Some candidates may be reluctant suitors of managers, but they are suitors nonetheless. They do not know where else to get the skills the managers claim to have and they are afraid to try to get along without them.

Additionally, many major funding sources for political campaigns now insist that good professional managers be retained for efforts they are supporting. One fund raiser who claims responsibility for about a million dollars a year for Republican candidates believes professional management is more important than the total amount of money spent in a campaign. As a result of this conviction, he reviews the management plans of any campaign that asks him for financial assistance. He says he has refused to raise money for some candidates solely because they did not have adequate professional management.

Other major donors to politics have begun to channel some of their money contributions to campaigns into professional services. Fearful that money would be poorly used, these donors have paid for campaign polls, consultants, media producers and sometimes full-time managers. This practice has been used with increasing frequency by both Republican and Democratic donors. Money, the most portable resource, used to be the best way for an outside force to intervene in an election. Professional managers, however, have succeeded in gaining recognition from donors that they, too, are a portable campaign resource that may be more valuable than money alone.

While their clients have come to recognize their authority, it is much harder to judge the broader community sanction that usually accompanies a group on its way to becoming a profession. The increasing role of professional managers is getting more public attention from mass news media. Newspapers and magazines throughout the country have carried stories about professional managers working in their areas on campaigns. A book about President Nixon's professional managers, *The Selling of the President*, 1968, was on the best-seller list for more than six months in 1970. While public attention cannot be equated with approbation, the increased recognition of professional managers' roles in campaigns has not created much of an outcry. The tone of most of the coverage recognizes the professional role of the managers.

Public displeasure has been directed against some of the techniques used by managers, especially television spots, but not against the managers. There has been increasing demand for regulation of the use of television in campaigns, but no attention to regulating the activities of the firms that encourage candidates to use massive amounts of television advertising. Further, none of the groups that pressed for campaign reforms has paid any attention to the campaign managers.

None has advocated, for example, that managers be required to file reports about their activities.

The managers are very concerned with their own public image. Its improvement was one of the reasons put forward in 1969 for establishing a professional association, which could help increase public understanding of the campaign managers' role in elections and counter a negative "image-maker" image. Hearing image-makers ponder their own images was quite humorous for some observers at the founding meeting of the American Association of Political Consultants, but they were deadly serious.

At least one of the managers said he was opposed to the creation of a professional association because it would merely confirm the negative ideas people had about managers as image manipulators. Others argued that increasing news media coverage of the role of managers was increasing public knowledge about them anyway. A professional association might lend some respectability to what they did, they argued, especially if it had an established code of ethics.

There was a consensus at the first meeting of the association that one of the things it would do would be help improve the image of professional campaign managers. In keeping with that desire, the board of the association passed a resolution favoring some limitation on the use of television advertising in campaigns. The managers had led candidates to spend more than 50 million dollars on television advertising in 1970.

The creation of the American Association of Political Consultants may help gain public recognition of the managers. However, its major contribution will be to the managers themselves. The act of creating a professional association moved the managers one giant irreversible step toward professionalism. The association is the brainchild and creature of four professional campaign managers—Joseph Napolitan, F. Clifton White, Martin Ryan Haley and Walter DeVries. It was established when they invited most of the campaign managers they knew about to a meeting at the Plaza Hotel in

New York in January, 1969. The same group had taken the lead a few months earlier in establishing an International Association of Political Campaign Consultants at a meeting in Paris.

About 50 people, who attended the first meeting in New York, heard the four founders tell them that the time had come for professional managers to be organized. "We've read about each other and read about the new techniques some of us use," they were told. Now it was time to have a group that could schedule seminars to examine the techniques used in campaigns and provide a forum for managers to exchange views.

A minority of those attending were not convinced that a professional association was needed or even possible. There was a long debate about the scope of the organization and about who would be in it. Would it include just people who managed campaigns full-time or could those who provide specialized services like film production join, too? What would be done about public affairs officers in corporations who became involved in campaigns every year on a part-time basis? How much experience would a person need before he would be allowed in? How are the professionals to be separated from the amateurs? The men who managed campaigns had come together to try to define who they were. The debate did not differ from the discussions in other groups on their way toward professionalism. For example, doctors still argue whether or not osteopaths should be counted in their profession. At the outset, all nascent professions try to draw boundaries that limit the number of people.

Several of the full-time managers argued for a very restricted definition of eligibility which would allow only people who actually earned their living planning and managing campaigns to become members of the association. Others contended that while the campaign was the common denominator of interest, there were many professionals, especially corporate public affairs officers, who spent only part of their time working on campaigns but who could benefit from membership in such an association.

Several of those who argued for a narrow definition of membership were afraid that membership in the association might be used by some as a credential to claim that they were professional managers when, in fact, they knew nothing. Others said they wanted an association of people who already knew something about campaign management rather than one that would let others join to learn what the business was all about. As one of them said: "I want people I can learn from. . . . I'm against an umbrella organization. I know as much about politics as most people. I want people here who will know more than me, not the public relations types."

In a debate that lasted several hours, two of the founders, Napolitan and White, suggested three categories of membership: regular membership for an elite composed of individuals who run political campaigns fairly regularly; associate membership for people who provide specialized services for campaigns such as film-making, polling and advertising; and academic membership for those in the academic community with an interest in political campaigns.

What the majority wanted was an elite of top managers, and the membership procedures that were finally adopted insured that result. Two categories of membership were established: full membership for those who managed campaigns full-time for a living and associate membership for those who provided specialized services to campaigns and academics with a particular interest in campaigns. The four founders were appointed to serve as a membership screening committee and the applications they sent out asked for detailed information about the applicant's major management responsibilities in five different campaigns. The first meeting also elected the founders as officers. Napolitan was elected president; White, vice president; Haley, treasurer; and DeVries, secretary. They set up various committees including program, by-laws, public relations and publications.

The association has continued its process of institutionaliza-tion. By the end of its second year, there were about 60 full paid-up members. At its 1971 meeting, it adopted a long set of by-laws to govern its operation and limit full participation to those the current members define as professional managers. The by-laws also set up a tight procedure under which the directors of the association can issue policy statements. The association began a quarterly professional journal, *Politeia*, which the second president of the association, White, hopes will become a major forum for communication between the practitioners of politics and scholars who study political be-havior. The association even did a survey of its own members to find out what kind of programs they wanted. The response was not very high, but the committee concluded that educa-tional programs were of greatest interest to the members.

By mid-1972, the association had conducted six major edu-cational seminars for professional campaign managers, four on recent developments in computers, television, polling and fund raising for campaigns, and two were reviews of some of the important 1970 and 1971 elections. About 150 attended each seminar.

The major problem for the association and for the managers who want recognition as professionals is the development of a code of ethics for the industry. At the first meeting, there was a heated debate about the desirability of establishing a code of ethics. Those who argued that ethics should be a principal concern of the association said that professional re-spect could never be achieved without a credible and enforce-able code. One of the proponents recalled the long discussion at the meeting about the managers' concern for their public image and said it was hard to believe the managers could not agree on some ethical standards for advertising and campaign finance.

A doubter in the back of the room shouted, "Good luck." Those who wanted the ethics questions soft-pedaled by the new association felt it would be impossible to get agreement on the subject. Further, they argued that if a tough set of standards was adopted, many managers would just stay outside the association and get all the business. Napolitan concluded the debate by expressing some sympathy for those concerned with ethics but said that he did not want the association to do anything that would interfere with a person's ability to make a living in campaigns. Besides, he added, the people he knew all had a high sense of ethics because they wanted to stay in business. Another founder, Martin Haley, suggested the Ten Commandments as an interim guide.

A committee, appointed to recommend a code, reported in March, 1971, that it was unable to agree on a set of guidelines. It recommended that in the meantime the association ask its members to adopt the pledge of the Fair Campaign Practices Committee, a mildly-worded promise to conduct a campaign in the highest American tradition of honesty. Most candidates sign the pledge at the beginning of the campaign and the voluntary Fair Campaign Practices Committee tries to investigate complaints of violations during the campaign. The recommendation was adopted.

The campaign management industry is young and its practitioners may develop a code of ethics. It took the Public Relations Society about ten years to develop a code of ethics its members would accept, and doctors have been fighting with each other for centuries about ethics. Nevertheless, until the managers make significant progress toward accepting a code of ethical behavior, their aspirations for full professional recognition will remain unsatisfied and the rest of us will remain nervous. They will have all the other aspects of a profession and still lack self-esteem and righteousness that come with having a well-advertised set of scruples.

CHAPTER 7

The Managers and the Political Parties

The reason the Republicans do not control the House of Representatives is poor campaign management. . . . Professional campaign management firms are the best thing that's ever happened to us. . . . I'd like every campaign person to get into the business.

> —*Jim Allison, a former official of the Republican National Committee who is now in a campaign management firm.*

The party could not provide these services in-house. The party is too weak. It is not trustworthy. No candidate could feel at ease with the party running things.

> —*Eugene Wyman, a former Democratic state chairman in California.*

I think a guy like Napolitan, with a tremendous capacity for self-promotion, hurts the candidates he works for. In 1966, Napolitan got more publicity than Shapp.

> —*A former official of the Democratic National Committee.*

I'd like the Senators to sit down and talk about it with a guy who really knows this business, like Napolitan. I don't like advertising agencies.

> —*An official of the Democratic Senatorial Campaign Committee in 1969.*

The contradictions between the managers' personal goals of professionalism and independence and the organizational need of a reliable source of business can be seen most clearly in

114

the relations between campaign management firms and political parties. The managers do not think very much of political parties, but their success is inextricably tied to the political parties.

Political parties have long been both a center of action and a focus of complaint for American politics. Social scientists have complained about the weakness and disorganization of American political parties at the same time they were saying party identification was the single best indicator of voting behavior. The professional campaign managers complain about the parties and talk about their independence from them, but in practice the managers can be seen clinging closer to the political parties than the voters. It is a case of "do as I say, not as I do." The managers write campaign material urging independence on the voters but align themselves with one party and stay there.

While the managers stay party bound, the voters seem to be returning to a 19th century American tradition of split-ticket voting. In the past five years, there has been a major shift away from personal party identification and straight party voting in American elections. Prior to 1966, people who identified strongly with one of the major political parties outnumbered those who called themselves independents by almost two to one. That ratio had remained almost unchanged for the 20 years that accurate data has been available from survey research polls. By 1969, there were fewer strong party identifiers than independents. Similarly, the percentage of people estimated to have voted a straight party ticket in state and local elections has fallen sharply from 60 percent and higher in most of the 20th century to 50 percent in 1966. This is a remarkable shift over a short period of time.

The professional managers, despite their views that parties are obsolete, have done no such moving around, however. More than 90 percent of the managers who participated in this study firmly identify themselves with a political party; 46 percent said they were Democrats and 41 percent identified themselves as Republicans. In the electorate as a whole, more than twice as many people call themselves Democrats than Republicans.

While the managers admitted to being party members, half of them said the party and ideological identification of their clients was unimportant. That is, they would work for someone they liked without regard to his party. However, what the managers said they would do and what they actually reported doing for the past ten years were very different things; 75 percent of the firms that supplied information about their campaign work in fact worked consistently for candidates from only one party. Of these, 48 percent of the firms reported working for Democrats only while 44 percent reported Republicans only. Only 25 firms reported campaigns that indicated any frequency of shifting back and forth between the parties. Most of the switching can be explained in ways that support the general conclusion that campaign management firms are very much part of the party family.

The discrepancy between what the managers said and what they did in campaigns is related to the managers' goal—and myth—of independence. Many of the professionals want to believe they have become free of the party. They could not sustain that belief, even to themselves, if they admitted from the outset that they were going to work for only one party. Further, as businessmen, most managers know it is hard to build up a steady flow of business switching back and forth. As professionals, however, they want to believe that they make their services available in a detached and objective way. To admit in advance that they would take only Republican or only Democratic campaigns would be inconsistent with the break from tradition they urge upon their clients and the voters. When a potential client from the other party calls upon a manager, some reason other than party can be found to turn him down.

The managers set up their firms to achieve independence and protection from the uncertainties of politics, but found out that the only way they could keep enough business coming in was to continue to affiliate with candidates of one political party. This is especially true for those who depend on their reputation among politicians to get new clients. There is surprisingly little interparty communication, so it is difficult to get known in both parties. In addition, the majority of the managers who work for one party had considerable previous experience in politics and were accustomed to the style and approach of that party. They would probably find themselves uncomfortable as well as unwelcome in the other party.

Even the firms that switched back and forth did not do so evenly. Only two firms in the entire study worked for an equal number of Democrats and Republicans. Ten worked for more Democrats than Republicans and 13 for more Republicans than Democrats. In most of the cases, the firm reported working for more than twice as many candidates in one party than the other.

Closer examination of the firms that reported working for substantial numbers of candidates in both parties strengthens rather then weakens the original conclusion that managers usually work for only one party. Most of the firms involved in the switching provided specialized services for campaigns but were not involved in management or counseling. For example, five of the 25 who switched regularly provided public opinion polling services only. One switcher was a radio and television time-buying consultant, two provided only computerized direct mail services, and another made films principally for Democrats but occasionally for liberal Republicans.

Others who reported working for both parties did so at different times or places. At least two of the firms that reported working for both parties began their business working for one party and then switched almost totally to the other. The owner of one of these firms said that he would now work for candidates he likes in either party. In fact, all of his clients in 1969 and 1970 were Democrats, but in 1971 he began working on a major 1972 Republican campaign.

Firms that cross party lines often run into hard times. For example, Baus & Ross worked for Republicans for more than 15 years but split with Ronald Reagan in 1966 and worked instead for the Democrat, Governor Edmund Brown. State Republican leaders said flatly in 1969 that they would not use the firm again in a major campaign, but Democratic leaders felt the firm was still Republican. In 1969, one of the partners had retired from the business to write crossword puzzle books and dictionaries and the other was contemplating whether or not to continue it. He did, but it now operates on a smaller base than before.

Some genuine party switching does occur but it is almost always along consistent ideological grounds. Several firms from the South, for example, reported working for Democrats in local and some statewide elections and Republicans in Senatorial and Presidential elections. In fact, several Southern firms that listed themselves as Democratic were suggested for inclusion in the study by state Republican chairmen who had been asked to name firms who had worked for Republican candidates.

Similarly, ideological switching occurs among some firms in the Northeast. For example, the owner of one firm said:

> We work for both parties. By inclination and in the past we worked for more Democrats. However, last year we worked for more liberal Republicans than Democrats. There is little distinction between the liberal Republicans and the liberal Democrats.

These firms may be reflective of a slight trend toward ideological realignment that is occurring in the South and the Northeast. However, they are still the exception among professional campaign firms, especially ones that are heavily involved in actual management and counseling.

The ability of the managers to operate successfully within the milieu of one political party depends in part upon the environment they find in the party and on the attitude of party professionals and candidates toward outside managers. While professional managers are generally accepted in both parties now, they play different roles in each. Most of these variations can be explained by recalling some of the obvious differences between the major political parties.

According to the registration figures, the Republican Party should almost never win an election. Less than one quarter of the electorate identifies itself as belonging to the Republican Party. In fact, there are now more "independents" than Republicans. While an increasing proportion of the electorate says it is independent of party and the people who say they are Democrats tend to vote less often, the Republicans know that they start most elections with a disadvantage. They know in advance that they have to convince people who are not Republicans to vote for their candidates if they are going to win.

At the national level, the Republicans have usually lost since 1932. The Republican Party has held the Presidency for 12 of the last 40 years and control of the Congress for only four of the last 40 years.

There has been more party competition, and Republican victory, at the state level. Except in the South, the Republican Party has regularly won control of governorships and state legislatures throughout the country. When this study began in 1969, the Republicans controlled 32 governorships; in 1972 they had 21. Most Republicans will admit that their party is almost non-existent in major cities; their strength is in the suburbs and rural areas.

However, without respect to whether they are in or out of power, the Republican Party does have at least the semblance of continuing organization at the national and state levels. Since the end of World War I, when the Republicans began setting up their unified finance effort, Republican finance committees have functioned in most states even if no Republicans held office. The structural base of the Republican

Party is in its continuing committees at the national and state level. The Republican National Committee and the Republican Senatorial and House Campaign Committees are in fact substantial organizations with large staffs and budgets. State Republican committees across the country have many more permanent employees than their Democratic counterparts.

What the Republicans have lacked in members and other resources they have usually been able to make up in money. Despite the fact that they have been out of power in the nation for most of the last 40 years, the Republican Party has consistently outspent the Democrats at virtually every level, with the possible exception of very recent Congressional elections.

The Republican Party has reached downward from its relatively well-financed committees to try to win votes in the precincts. Because its local organizations and popular membership have been so weak, it has needed to find a way to turn its money resources into campaign resources that could win votes from non-Republicans. Professional campaign managers lend themselves readily to helping solve this problem. Their geographic mobility and capability of working without a previously existing party structure allows the Republican Party to use firms in areas it thinks it can win, even if the party base is weak.

Additionally, the leadership of the Republican finance committees and the party itself is still drawn largely from business executives, who have become accustomed to solving problems by bringing in consultants from the outside. One national Republican official interviewed for this study felt the use of private campaign management and consulting organizations was fully analogous to their use in business. People on the staff become too attuned to what is going on inside, he said. The consultants can bring new ideas in from the outside.

For these reasons the Republican Party has been favorably disposed to use of professional campaign managers and consultants in recent years. This has been especially true at the national level in connection with Congressional elections. Elections to individual seats in the House of Representatives are essentially local affairs. To win control of the House, a party must be able to win 218 different elections. In their attempt to gain control of the Congress, the Republican Party has tried to impose organization and campaign resources from the top to make up for its local weakness. It has done this, in part, through professional campaign management firms for several years, but national level intervention in Republican campaigns for Congress was especially marked in 1968 and 1970.

For the 1968 elections, the Republican National Campaign Committees commissioned public opinion polls and other basic demographic research for districts they considered to be marginal. They used this information, collected by a pool of professional campaign management and polling firms, as the basis for recruiting candidates and planning campaigns. A similar polling effort preceded the 1970 elections, when the President himself urged some people to run with professional help.

During the 1960's, the Republican Congressional Committees established a "credit" system to impose some control on the money they invested in local districts to win a House or Senate seat. Candidates used their credits for things like research, professional campaign management or consulting and campaign advertising. The system was adopted to try to get candidates to spend money for professional campaign services rather than rely on amateurs and friends who might not know anything about political campaigns.

In mid-1971, at least some national-level Republicans had begun to question sharply the party's approach to national and Congressional campaigning. The results, they argued, did not nearly match the money that had been invested in campaigns, especially for the Congress. Between 1966 and 1970, the national-level Republican Congressional Booster and Senatorial Campaign Committees reported spending more than 12 million dollars and a good deal of additional money was given directly to candidates at the request of the committees without being entered on the committees' books. The results have not been as impressive as the effort. Before the 1964 elections, there were 258 Democrats and 176 Republicans in the House and 68 Democrats and 32 Republicans in the Senate. Six years and many million dollars later, the Republicans had a net gain of four seats in the House and 13 seats in the Senate. Throughout the period, the use of professional managers had grown remarkably, especially for House elections, and some people wondered what they had accomplished.

It is not clear that this skepticism will actually hurt the campaign managers. Their rejoinder to party critics is there are still not enough campaign managers to make a dent. If there were more good managers, the results would be better, they argue. Further, the incumbent in a Congressional election starts so far ahead of any challenger that there are few things short of getting caught in bed with his male secretary that could make him lose. The average incumbent in the House begins the election campaign with resources valued between $16,000 and $50,000 that are just not available to his challenger. He has government staff, offices and phones, he has a free mailing allowance and he can use his public office to get on television news programs in his district almost any time he wants. His challenger must use money to get any or all of these. Even with the best professional management it is unlikely that the Republicans will be able to take control of the House of Representatives. Under the current rules of the game, control of the Congress could change only with a basic and massive shift in voter alignment and attitudes. That does not happen very often and is not caused by clever campaign techniques. Thus, despite the new skepticism, national-level Republicans are continuing to rely on professional management firms for help in Congressional elections.

At the state level, where Republicans have had power more frequently, attitudes toward the professional managers are more mixed. Republican governors have often declined to use firms because they have had enough trained professionals on their state staffs. One Republican state party official in California interviewed for this study felt that while the firms then under contract to the state committee were invaluable aids, their true worth had never been tested because "they have been competing against nothing [on the Democratic side]." He said that for the long term, he favored the development of in-house campaign management and consulting capabilities. An official at the local level, however, complained that there still were not enough professional campaign management firms to work for Republican candidates.

In general, Republican candidates and officials were more willing to assign broad strategic and operational responsibilities to management firms than their Democratic counterparts were. If they were willing or anxious to use firms—as they were at the national level—they were willing to turn most of the responsibility over to them.

The Democratic Party is still the majority party in the nation. It has enjoyed a substantial registration and identification advantage over the Republicans, and, if early trends in youth registration are maintained, the Democrats will have an even greater advantage in the future. For the past 40 years, Democrats at the national level have usually won.

At the state level, the Democrats have had almost a monopoly of power in the South for the last hundred years but have regularly shared power with the Republicans in most other areas of the country. The core of the Democratic majority remains in the nation's large cities even if the old Democratic organizations are weak and many of the precinct workers' children live in the suburbs. However, the new immigrants to the cities, the blacks, vote even more heavily Democratic than the people they are replacing. In the suburbs, however, the Democrats have neither a history of power nor much organization.

Democratic Party leaders argue that they do not have the

same continuing financial and organizational base that the Republicans enjoy. They believe the power and heart of the Democratic Party structure rests with its elected office holders. If there were no Democrats in power, said one, there would be no Democratic Party.

In many senses this is true. The party as an organization is heavily dependent on being in office. The Republicans have usually outspent the Democrats but the Democrats have been able to use the advantages and resources available to them as the controllers of government. In the classic form of Democratic organization, the urban machine, most of the party workers were on the public payroll. Similarly, the Democrats in power at the national level have developed considerable political resources. It is no accident that since 1952 more than 90 percent of all House members running for re-election have won.

Since the party leadership has usually been drawn from people who hold power, Democratic leaders have perceived less of a need for independent outside help in organizing and running campaigns than the Republicans. They have used their own past victories as evidence that they did not need help in winning future victory. However, Democratic strength in the Senate has been eroded in the past several elections. By 1969, the leadership there was anxious for outside professional help. Members of the House still seemed content to use their office staff to plan and run elections. Many House members who have not run a real campaign for re-election in 15 or 20 years are shocked when they are told that some people spend $250,000 on a campaign for the House.

At the state level, the attitude toward professional campaign managers is also mixed. In large areas of the South, public relations and professional campaign management firms have been used for some time as an alternative to developing any real party organization. In other areas of the country, the attitude toward professional management has usually varied depending on how recently the Democrats held power in the state. Where the Democrats have been out of power and the state party organization is a shambles, self-starting candidates for state office have turned to professional managers to plan and run campaigns. If they win, the party is revived with people sympathetic to outside managers. Where the Democrats have been in power for some time, the leaders have been more hostile to outsiders running campaigns; rather, they have viewed professional managers as specialists in some aspect of campaigning, especially media. They are unwilling to assign broad responsibility to managers. In the cities, traditional party leaders have also been opposed to outside management firms. Even where the organization's strength has been eroded by time and population changes, the Democratic chieftains do not want outside help. To them, loyalty to the party leader remains the most important asset of a party worker. The managers do not qualify.

Despite this hostility from party leaders, the professional managers have made considerable headway inside the Democratic Party and have been active in almost as many Democratic campaigns as Republican. However, the grand total conceals important differences in the parties. The Democrats have a much greater recent history of insurgency within the party; Democrats fight with each other in primaries more frequently than Republicans do. Thus, the management firms have a particular role for the primary battles of Democrats. The firms that work for Democrats reported heavier involvement in primaries than in general elections while the reverse was true for the Republicans.

Further, when Democratic Party leaders talk about professional managers, they usually mean media or research specialists. The Democrats think of the managers as specialists with important but narrow responsibilities in campaigns. Democratic Party leaders and their principal supporters within the labor movement believe that key strategic decisions must remain in party hands.

While the Republicans are generally viewed as being more

"modern" than the Democrats in their approach to communications and research, the Democrats have made use of modern communications devices for years. They used film for political propaganda purposes as early as 1918 when Bernard Baruch financed a film designed to help the Democrats sell the public on joining the League of Nations. Franklin Delano Roosevelt fully exploited the political potential of radio when he used his mellifluous voice to soothe the aches and pains of millions of people who did not have enough to eat. Adlai E. Stevenson made early use of television when he booked half-hour segments on national television to talk his sense to the American people. The appearances were not slick or smooth but he tried.

Democratic Party leaders, however, view all this communication activity as an addition to their traditional campaign efforts. They may be kidding themselves about the extent and effectiveness of the traditional party campaign effort but it remains important in the minds of the party leaders.

Few observers think that American political parties are doing a very good job. However, that is not why the professional managers dislike them. They view parties only as mechanisms for running elections. One manager summarized the feelings of his colleagues well:

> American parties are doing an atrocious job, if you define the job as aiding and reelecting their members . . . So much is known about politics and how to elect people but . . . it isn't used. One of the problems is the people who work for the committees. You can't find sharp people to work for non-profit organizations so the people at the committees aren't that good.

At least one of the major professional managers, Matt Reese, tries to beat the traditional patronage organizations at their own game, organizing at the precinct level. He likes to tell the story about the big city ward leader who would not let his firm operate in his district during a mayoral primary. The firm worked successfully in other areas of the city and after the election the ward leader came around to see how and why they did so well. At that point in the story, the manager always smiles and says: "Most of those guys didn't have lists, or organizations. They were phonies. We got 15,000 people to work in the campaign." That is true, but it is not political organization either. Asked whether all these instant volunteers stayed active after the election, he replied: "I don't know, I haven't been there. My consulting fee stopped on Election Day."

From the professional managers' point of view, political parties should concentrate on winning elections, little else. They do not recognize other political roles for parties as being important. Several complained that internal party disputes over policy and ideology just got in the way of electoral success. None mentioned the party as a link between the individual citizen and government. Only a few made mention of the party as the basis of organizing government. Again, the professionals' perspective is limited because they are not interested in government or policy. The few managers who had complimentary views of the parties made the point. Several managers felt the parties were adapting very quickly to their point of view about politics and the role of the party in it.

The professional managers do not perceive themselves to be replacements for local parties, but they do think they are an alternative to relying on parties for elections. This is especially true for rich candidates. As one of the more direct managers put it, "Only people who are intelligent and rich call me."

The view of the professional that campaigns are games and businesses that ought to be run in business-like fashion extends to their view of political parties. From Whitaker and Baxter to the firms that are opening today, professional campaign managers have had a negative view of the political parties and the people who toil in them. Clem Whitaker Sr. once wrote that he thought there were too many political organizations.

The views of current managers are not very much changed. One said that he disliked both parties, and that the only things he wanted to know about a candidate were whether or not he was a winner and whether he could pay. Local parties are, he said, "six guys who think they are the party. What clowns!" Another said that while he thought the Republicans were better organized than the Democrats in his state, it was like comparing two college sophomores. A third said that the parties were "doing a lousy job. They are wandering around in the past. They don't know if they have a constituency or how to reach it." The majority of managers who participated in this study said the parties were weak now and were getting weaker all the time. And, 86 percent of the managers felt they made up for weakness in local parties and 39 percent thought it was accurate to say that they "protect the candidate from his friends in his own organization and in his political party."

Managers have little respect for precinct organizations. One said that the computer had made precinct politics outdated. Another argued that "the principal vehicle of politics has changed from parties to television."

The managers' view that elections are a business also affects their attitudes toward candidates. They know there is a difference between selling a candidate and selling toothpaste, but, the candidate is a product, nonetheless. For most managers, the candidate is a thing about which a favorable name recognition must be built, a thing to be moved from place to place in the district and displayed on television, a focus of activity, but, in fact, not central in the campaign. The candidate is just one actor in the professional managers' plans.

One of the principal criteria the managers reported using in deciding who to work for was whether or not the candidate would do what he was told. Almost all of the managers demand complete access to the candidate at any time during the campaign, but many keep their distance most of the time. A few say they try to have as little to do with the candidate as possible. One major firm has changed its approach to supplying services without direct consulting to avoid dealing with individual candidates. One of the managers admitted that he stays away from the candidate because "I've got things to do" and "he needs to think I am a miracle man." He continued: "Most candidates are bores anyway. They're not my kind of people."

The managers believe that they understand the needs of the campaign much better than the candidate. Indeed they may. Most professional managers have been involved in many more campaigns than the candidates. They think that candidates who interfere with running the campaigns are foolish and they resent the amateurism of candidates.

Few managers are as contemptuous of their clients as the one who advises his candidates to go away and hide while he puts on their campaign. This manager bragged that he had a candidate in Georgia once who he told to go to Seal Island until after the election. He said his firm does not charge clients for arranging personal appearances because he does not believe in them. "When they make speeches in public they just get in trouble," he complained. He argues that elections are a market in which you can get a list of all the "buyers." You find out what they want through survey research and then you give it to them in the form of a packaged product, the candidate. It's simple, he says, but "the dumbbells in politics" don't know it.

The managers in search of professional status and recognition do not want candidate-clients who will be an embarrassment to them among their colleagues in politics. Therefore, their perception of the ideal candidate for public office is different from others'. They try to avoid candidates who will not take their advice or who look stiff on television or who insist on making public statements that might "hurt the campaign." They must be people who "understand" modern communications and who can pay for it. They must be personally attractive or at least salable in both looks and personality. Another characteristic that managers cited repeatedly was that their candidate-clients had to be "reasonable" people, both in their political views and in their personal behavior. They must be people the managers can "get along with." In this subtle way, the managers are beginning to set standards about who is an "acceptable" candidate. Some of the managers think the public should be grateful to them for weeding "charlatans" and "jerks" out of political campaigns.

The motivations and goals of the managers also affect their view of the electorate. They are the buyers to whom the candidates must be sold. The majority of managers view the electorate as a pliable but uninterested mass. They believe their techniques are "persuading people and changing people's political decisions."

The professional managers are not very interested in issues themselves and they transpose that lack of interest to the voters. Many argue that modern problems are so complex that it is impossible for anyone, let alone the average voter, to understand them. Therefore, they try to stay away from issues in campaigns. Today's managers generally agree with Whitaker's belief that the voters would just as soon see a fight as a debate between the candidates.

Treleaven's view about the role of issues in campaigns and the attitudes of voters toward issues is typical for the managers as a whole. He does not see why issues have to be involved in selling a candidate at all. In his report on the Bush for Congress campaign which he ran in 1966, Treleaven wrote, "Most issues today are so complicated, so difficult to understand, and to have opinions on that they either intimidate or, more often, bore the average voter." Treleaven and his colleagues decided to sell Bush as a fighting underdog because people would sympathize with that. There were no other issues. Bush won that election, but he lost a Senate race two years later using the same team of managers.

Many managers try to develop single themes for their campaigns that go beyond politics. Themes used in the 1970 elections are good examples. Buckley in New York used "Stand up for America." The basic ad was a 60-second jingle with pictures of a smiling Buckley shaking hands with all kinds of voters. Ottinger's manager used: "Ottinger Delivers." Cannon in Nevada was a man who "cares." In Utah, the Republican managers ran Burton for Senate as "A Man to Match the Mountains." Campaign themes are supposed to be evocative of sympathy and support, but virtually content free. In the view of the managers, the voters won't know or care about substance.

Lincoln defined democracy as the system that was of, by and for the people. The professional campaign managers see things differently. They look at politics as professional athletes might look at their sport; they are getting paid to play a game they like. They have made a business of politics because they like politics, not because they like or dislike people or government. They need not care about the quality or even quantity of mass participation in the elections they run.

Like athletes, they are interested only in the short-term result, winning the election at hand. They think that worrying about the process of democracy or the democratic functions of elections that go beyond picking a set of temporary leaders is all "make work" to keep political scientists and journalists off the unemployment rolls. Bill Roberts of Spencer-Roberts made this quite clear when he addressed a group of campaign managers at a training program sponsored by the Republican National Committee:

> As a campaign manager, your sole purpose is to win. There is absolutely no other goal. You are not trying to prove a cause or sell a philosophy. You are trying to win a campaign in the most expeditious manner possible, using every legal and moral way to do so.

Questions about democracy and the place of elections in it do not bother the professional managers because of their perspective on elections. To them, elections are a game and a business. They view the election as a unit in space and time removed from the rest of what happens in our public life. It is not their business to calculate the possible impact of what they do in an election on future policy or governmental actions any more than it is the professional football player's problem to worry about the impact of football on people's attitudes toward violence and aggression.

In 1964, Johnson ran for President as the "Peace Candidate," and his campaign strategy played heavily on convincing the American people that Goldwater was a war-monger. To make sure no one missed the point, Johnson's media advisors created a spot television ad in which a little girl was shown picking flowers until a nuclear bomb went off in the background. It was a fine piece of art and its creators were quite proud of it, but it probably did not have much effect on the election; Johnson had won long before any active campaigning began. Nevertheless, the Johnson campaign had a large amount of money which the managers wanted to spend and they wanted to leave no doubt that Goldwater would be dangerous.

It is possible to argue that the long-term impact of the 1964 campaign has weakened the political system's ability to deal with questions of war and peace in electoral campaigns, lowered the credibility of politicians in general and contributed to a climate of suspicion and distrust that is clouding our politics. One of the reasons the Pentagon Papers had such an impact was the widespread belief that the campaign of 1964 had been deliberately deceptive. The peace and anti-war theme was attractive in 1964, but it left Johnson and the leaders of the Democratic Party, indeed most elected politicians, with mud on their faces and blood on their hands. Predicting Armageddon is often a tempting short-term tactic, but when it does not happen or when you do exactly what you predicted the other fellow would do, you are caught in a trap that encourages further deception and even more dire predictions. But this trap does not snare the professional managers because they are gone after Election Day.

The vast majority of professional campaign managers believe that one of their contributions to campaigns is their "objective" point of view. They may well take a detached and experienced look at the campaigns in which they work, but that view is far from objective. Like everyone else, the managers' perception of what they look at is colored and distorted by their image of what they want. As has been shown here, their motivations and goals give them a view of politics and its participants that differs sharply from our traditional notions of the part elections ought to play in democratic life.

The campaign management industry is still quite young and while it has been growing with almost unbelievable speed, it is not yet clear that the managers will be able to achieve their goals through private profit-making firms. In fact, there is some doubt on the long-term viability of the industry. However, if managers do succeed, even in the short term, they may well leave the political system weaker and less democratic than they found it. Elections may be fulfilling and profitable for the managers, but not for the rest of us who think the political system ought to help solve some of the real problems we face.

CHAPTER 8
Will They Survive?

We had no customers on November 6. There hasn't
been the slightest help to keep us in business, not even
referrals. There may be enough [business in campaigns
alone] for an itinerant individual, but not for an
organization.
> —*An owner of a campaign management
> firm in mid-1969.*

Between the primary and the general I paid six professionals to sit home and wait until I got business for
the general. . . . I still have trouble meeting the payroll.
> —*An owner of a campaign management
> firm.*

What off season?
> —*A busy campaign manager in mid-1969.*

The professional campaign managers established their firms
to overcome some of the uncertainties of electoral politics
and by so doing they created whole new sets of problems
for themselves. These may be at least as vexing as the troubles
they faced in their previous political or commercial work.
With the possible exception of Whitaker and Baxter, no campaign management firm has survived the departure of its
founders. So far, the firms have provided short-term protection for their founders, but all have been overcome by the
problems of building and maintaining institutions. Those who
have made the most determined efforts to build institutions
have found that their original goals for going into the business
have been compromised or abandoned and have been sup-
planted by new organizationally-related goals.

Organizations, like organic systems, require care and feed-
ing; they do not survive without it. In this respect, a campaign

management firm with five employees faces the same problems as General Motors with hundreds of thousands of employees. In larger organizations, formal subdivisions are assigned different activities or roles and each can be identified and analyzed by itself. In a small organization, like a professional campaign management firm, one or two partners may play all the roles. Formal subdivisions may not exist in a small organization, but the activities associated with each essential task must be accomplished. All organizations must carry on at least five essential activities to overcome the natural tendency to die.

In order to survive, an organization needs: 1) a production system to make a product or provide a service, 2) a support system to market whatever is produced and acquire new resources, 3) a maintenance system to keep the organization and its people working together, 4) an adaptation system to keep up external changes in the environment or the technology of the business, and 5) a managerial system to run the whole enterprise. All of these functions are obvious, but it is useful to list them to help understand the kinds of problems the professional managers must solve to make their firms successful. These five realities of organization force the managers to cope with specific problems of production, marketing and management.

The firms must overcome limitations in the production of the services they provide to campaigners. At the outset, most campaign management firms have only the time of their principals to sell. That is limited, and the firm must often go outside itself through subcontracting to other firms to meet its obligations to a specific campaign. Firms that have nothing to sell but the time of a few key people are permanently limited. They cannot grow beyond the physical capacities of their top people.

The usual way for organizations to overcome the tendency to decay is to grow both horizontally and vertically, that is, to get bigger and to add new and different services. The campaign management firms that have survived the longest have followed both courses. They grew horizontally by expanding the geographic areas in which they worked and by increasing the number of campaigns they handled at the same time. They expanded vertically by adding additional specialized service capabilities and by developing non-campaign capabilities. Most of the campaign management firms to date have expanded only by having the principals work on more and more campaigns each season. This solution to the problem of growth is not good for the health of either the individuals involved or the institutions they are trying to build. At some relatively low point, the individual reaches his physical and mental limit. If the firm has nothing else to offer, it has no way of bringing new resources in to replace what is being burned up in the frantic activity of the principal managers. That is why so few firms last.

Whitaker and Baxter survived because it grew both horizontally and vertically. In addition to offering campaign services to candidates, the firm managed campaigns for ballot propositions in California and occasional campaigns outside the state. It opened a large office in Chicago during the late 1940's to manage the American Medical Association's nationwide campaign against national health insurance. The key to its longevity, however, was its ancillary services—the weekly news service, the political public relations work for commercial clients, and, especially, the advertising agency that collected all those commissions. Even so, the firm's dominance of California Republican politics ended with the departure of Clem Whitaker Sr. and Leone Baxter. The firm continued into the 1970's under the direction of Clem Whitaker Jr. and several other partners, growing horizontally. To make up for the loss of dominance in California, the firm became more heavily involved in political campaigns outside the state; for example, the firm worked for Senator Griffen in Michigan in recent years. It also expanded its political work for corporations and professional associations.

The firm of Spencer-Roberts also tried to overcome the problems of entropy through horizontal and vertical growth. In the late 1960's and early '70's, the firm sought some political campaigns outside California. It managed or counseled campaigns in Washington state, Michigan, Arizona, Georgia, Hawaii and other states to gain a nationwide clientele and reputation. The horizontal growth of the firm within the state was somewhat limited by a provision in its contract with the Republican State Committee, which gave the state party virtual veto power over campaigns the company handled within the state. Even so, the number of California campaigns the firm handled increased, too. In 1970, the firm managed or consulted in the gubernatorial, senatorial and state legislative elections in California. Spencer himself managed at least five state assembly races and was principal consultant on the Reagan campaign and several races outside California.

Spencer-Roberts expanded vertically in 1966 by creating an electronic data processing subsidiary, Datamatics, and again in 1970 by creating the Spencer-Roberts Advertising Company to handle advertising for its campaigns. This kind of growth was designed to keep the firm up to date with changes in the environment and technology.

The recent breakup of Spencer-Roberts and its subsidiary, Decision Making Information, described earlier, can be explained in part by the organizational problem of growth. The firm originally created a small subsidiary, Datamatics, to do its data processing and its demographic research. However, once created, the subsidiary itself had to face the realities of organization, and in 1969, was reorganized and expanded to include a polling capability. This addition allowed it to make greater use of its demographic and statistical research as well as provide a new service to potential customers. The firm remained related to Spencer-Roberts. During the 1970 campaigns, however, the principals of the subsidiary wanted to expand again to provide political counseling on their own and to place some of their advertising with a firm other than

Spencer-Roberts Advertising. The firm also wanted to do some non-political work. Thus, by trying to solve some of its own problems through growth, the subsidiary came into direct conflict with its parent company. This conflict, coupled with other emerging problems, led to the separation of the two firms in early 1971.

A second problem that the realities of organization force upon the professional managers is the constant need to get new business. Firms must relate to their environment in a way that will bring them new campaigns or other business if the campaign work is not sufficient to meet the costs. This is, of course, an obvious solution, but that does not mean it is an easy one. Even some of the successful companies have a hard time meeting their expenses between campaign seasons. Virtually all of the managers set up their firms bullish about the prospects for future business and most of the firms have at least some prior arrangements for the first few campaigns. It is only after the first or second campaign season that they begin to face the problem of finding enough new business to meet expenses. Few of them do what they advise their clients to do: long-range market planning.

If the managers are to be taken at their word, they campaign for business the way McKinley campaigned for the Presidency—they sit and wait for people to come to them. Almost 85 percent of the managers reported that they were usually hired after being contacted by the candidate or members of his campaign committee. In interviews, managers stressed that candidates got in touch because of their reputation. Recommendations from past clients were viewed as particularly helpful by several managers. As one manager said: "Most of my business comes from referrals . . . There are so few of us in the business that a little success brings the business in . . ." Relying on reputation and past record for marketing means that managers make next year's marketing decisions by deciding which campaigns to work in this year.

While the managers are usually hired directly by the candidate or his committee, others sometimes act as middlemen. National, state or local party organizations sometimes hire firms or request them to work for candidates in target areas. One of the lures President Nixon used to convince people to run for the Senate in 1970 was a promise of professional campaign management. Several of the key managers from Nixon's 1968 campaign were involved in the Senate races in 1970 at the request of the White House.

State and local party organizations also hire firms directly themselves. That was the case with Spencer-Roberts and Calplan, the long-term project to take control of the state legislature by the Republicans in California in 1970. The state committee assigned the firm to work on special elections to fill vacated seats and on target races during the general election. The state Republican committee in Texas also retained management firms to help run legislative races in that state. A similar plan was proposed to the New York Democratic Legislative Campaign Committee for key state legislative seats in 1970 by Campaign Planners, Inc., the campaign subsidiary of the Lennen and Newell advertising agency.

County committees sometimes hire firms, too. Matt Reese's first major client was a county level organization in Jackson County, Missouri. The Citizens for County Progress there began as a reform group challenging the incumbent county committee. When it gained control of the county, it continued to retain Reese's consulting services. Another manager told of an instance when his company was hired by a county committee to run a campaign for county executive. The candidate wanted nothing to do with the firm but since the county chairman controlled the money, the candidate had little choice. He won the election.

About half the managers said they never solicited candidates, and only 9 percent said their business always came from direct solicitation. The managers argue that there are good reasons for this kind of passive marketing program. They do not think it is professional to solicit business openly. Managers believe that if they have to "sell" a candidate they will be at a disadvantage in getting him to follow their advice. As one of them said:

> The company policy is never to solicit candidates. The relationship between a manager and a client is strange. They have to respect you. They have to want you bad enough to listen. If you've solicited them, the situation becomes unmanageable.

While managers frown on direct solicitation, there are important forms of indirect solicitation engaged in rather openly. They advertise themselves and their services by participating in campaign management and planning seminars held across the country by political parties, corporations and groups like the Chamber of Commerce. These seminars give the managers an opportunity to show themselves off, a chance to sell their own views about how politics and elections ought to be run and in some cases an opportunity to make some quick money.

The Republican National Committee conducted a series of regional campaign management and planning seminars for party leaders throughout the country during the late 1960's and early 1970's. Most of the substantive presentations were given by representatives of professional management firms. Spencer-Roberts, for example, developed a formal training program for campaign managers that included a full campaign planning simulation game. The material for the course and game was drawn from actual campaigns the company had run and showed clearly what the company could do for a candidate. When the seminar series began, the Republican National Committee paid the managers to make presentations, which helped some of the companies get through the off-season. However, the appearances proved to be such successful marketing devices for the firms that payments for appearances has been stopped. Now, the companies make presentations for nothing.

Managers who work for Democrats have been at something

of a disadvantage because the party has not had a similar series of seminars. They have had a more difficult time displaying their talents and achievements and meeting potential candidates and clients long before the election period. Several of the Democratic managers complained that they often had trouble finding out early enough who was planning to run for a given office.

In recent years, however, the ability of Democrats to show themselves off has been increasing. The Democratic Senatorial Campaign Committee, for example, sponsored a campaign planning seminar for the aides of members running for re-election in 1970. About 100 people attended to hear presentations by several of the Democratic management firms and to see some of the materials the firms had produced in past campaigns. One manager reported that he received between 15 and 20 calls from potential clients as a result of his appearance at the seminar.

Some of the firms work hard to cultivate good working relationships with national, state and local party organizations to help get campaign contracts and work between campaigns. This approach to marketing is not without risks to the independence that the managers are seeking. A firm that is close to one set of leaders may find itself without work in that area if its patrons lose control or it may find that it is unable to accept work it would otherwise take because its friends in the party object. One firm, for example, was asked to run a primary contest in Buffalo for a candidate it liked against someone it did not like. The company turned down the offer because it feared it would jeopardize the relationship it had established with the county chairman and therefore interfere with future job possibilities in the county.

Some firms have also developed working relationships with private political interest groups. More than half the firms that cooperated in this study said they had been asked to do political work by private interest groups and by their commercial clients. In some cases, the firms were hired by the commercial companies and paid with company funds to do political campaign work. This is a clear violation of the federal election laws, and several campaign management firms have been caught and fined for taking money from corporations and then using it in political campaigns. Such money is deemed to be a contribution from the corporation to the campaign. The recent prosecutions of several firms in California have made managers quite wary about using or discussing this method of getting corporate money into campaigns. However, the practice continues.

The corporations and associations that run political education workshops and seminars usually still pay. Educational programs are an easy and legal way for groups to get money to firms and politicians they like. They hire the firm to give a short seminar and pay it a very high price and the firm sometimes hires a public office holder to make a presentation. Spencer-Roberts has been reported to get as much as $5,000 for a two-day seminar put on by three people.

The American Medical Political Action Committee, the political arm of the American Medical Association, has probably been the largest private user of professional campaign management firms. It has used firms to help find districts in which candidates for Congress who were friendly to AMA positions might win, and it has used firms to help elect friendly candidates. AMPAC and its state level committees are now one of the largest contributors to political campaigns in the nation. Organized doctors were reported to have contributed between 3.5 and four million dollars in 1968 and more than five million dollars to the 1970 campaigns.

One manager is meeting some of his organizational costs by working for Common Cause, helping it set up a telephone communication network among its members and volunteers and advising on its election reform and voter registration programs. Another manager relied on a contract with the Citizens' Committee for Public Broadcasting to carry his company for its first five months.

Several managers believe they and their colleagues will be hired more and more frequently by private political interest groups because they provide a tool for intervention in politics that is too tempting to pass up for a group that is vitally concerned about the outcome of an election. As campaign costs have skyrocketed in recent years, major donors have become quite anxious about the way their money is used. Mistakes are quite costly. A poorly-done poll can cost the donors $10,000 and be useless or $50,000 can be spent to produce television commercials that cannot be run because they say the wrong things. To prevent this, the donors are turning to the management firms.

Thus, Baus & Ross did political research for a group of third-class mail users to suggest ways it might defeat incumbent Senator Mike Monroney, who opposed its interests when he was Chairman of the Senate Post Office Committee. During the campaign, the mailers told the firm to do what it could to help the challenger; the incumbent lost. An owner of this firm said there were many other instances in which an interested group had hired his company to achieve some political end:

> We have always been allied with business and industry, putting over things they wanted. At times, they get involved in a candidate. When they do, party doesn't matter. When we represented a Democrat, it was usually a story like this. We represented Sam Yorty in a race for Congress in 1949. He wanted state ownership of the tideland oil deposits so the petroleum group wanted him. They asked us to work for him.

Becoming too heavily involved with one party committee or one special interest group may cause new problems for managers when they face the organizational reality of finding a reliable source for new business. Most of the firms try to protect their independence by seeking work with several different party committees or interest groups. A few succeed. Others, fearful of getting trapped with a party faction or single interest group, look for campaigns to run all the time or try to find other kinds of business to fill in between the campaigns.

The emergence of the American Association of Political Consultants and its publication, *Politeia*, have also given managers a new opportunity to display their work before potential customers. The seminars sponsored by the association are largely for the education of its members, but they are usually attended by party officials, members of candidates' staffs and journalists. In a seminar following the 1970 elections, managers from leading races all over the country told each other and the eagerly listening press how "they elected"—or tried to elect—various candidates. Party officials responsible for planning 1972 campaigns sat in the audience and took careful notes. Members of the press found the stories so interesting they wrote about them, and were effectively barred from future seminars of the association.

It is becoming easier for the firms to find year-round campaign work, a dramatic development of the last three years. In 1969, major management firms were involved in many more local elections than ever before. One Los Angeles candidate for the county Junior College Board paid a firm $30,000 to run his campaign, clearly planning to use it as a stepping-stone to higher office. Another firm did television consulting in a city as small as Reading, Pennsylvania, for about the same fee it charged in larger races. Further, almost all of the major firms had signed contracts for at least some 1970 campaigns by June, 1969. The same was true in mid-1971 for 1972. By July, most of the firms had begun paid planning of the 1972 races. Extensive research and strategy writing were occupying some companies full-time. Matt Reese had a contract to write formal campaign plans for Presidential primaries in eight states but the candidate withdrew early in the game. Bob Squier had a contract that called for half-time consulting to Edmund Muskie through 1971 and then full-time for 1972.

Polling firms had also begun work on the 1972 elections early in 1971.

It would not be unreasonable to estimate that more than ten million dollars was spent on the 1972 campaigns during 1971, a good deal of it going to professional campaign management firms for research and planning. If this level of off-year spending continues, most of the firms will be able to work on campaigns year-round.

Some firms turn to public relations or advertising work between campaigns either because they have to in order to meet the costs of running organizations or because they enjoy the variety and use the period to rejuvenate themselves. Some of the managers say that their commercial work has absolutely nothing to do with their political work. For them, working in politics sometimes makes it difficult to get commercial public relations, governmental counseling or advertising work. Many companies are reluctant to use their firms, managers complain, because they fear the commercial work will not get proper attention if something interesting comes along in politics. Other corporations are wary about becoming involved with a public relations or counseling firm that itself might be a matter of political controversy. However, for the managers who are not troubled by trading on their political connections and experience, lobbying and political consulting for corporate clients can be a very profitable way to fill the time between elections.

One of the best sources of information about campaign managers in one state was the political lobbyist for a major bank, who said he dealt with the managers all the time when he needed things done. A few of the managers seem to revel in the "fix-it" role that has been traditionally ascribed to ward leaders and political bosses, despite all their pronouncements against the patronage politics of the past. One manager who likes the wheeling and dealing works for Democratic candidates during the campaign season and represents heavily-regulated industries like public utilities during the off-season. He said he sometimes charges the industries on the basis of the results he gets for them. Another, who did much the same thing for Republicans, claimed he charged only for getting clients "in the door" to make their case, not for the results. A third manager, whose firm actually does more lobbying than campaign management, saw no conflict between his activities as a manager and campaign fund raiser and his work as a governmental affairs representative:

> I am in the business of dealing with government. So, if I can help people get elected, it helps me in my other work. All my clients are in businesses with close connections to politics. They give heavily.

To some of the campaign management firms, old-fashioned political patronage from friends and past clients is the base of their survival for the off-season. This is particularly true in California, where mayors and governors have a lot to say about which firms handle public relations for things like school and bond referenda.

The Nixon Administration has tried to use some of its considerable patronage to help professional managers it likes. Treleaven is a case in point. Treleaven did yeoman service for the Republicans in 1970; he did not have a lot of winners but he handled some of the toughest races. He would be busy again in 1972, but in the meantime he needed something to do. When Rogers C. B. Morton resigned as Republican National Chairman to become Secretary of the Interior, a niche was found for Treleaven. Jim Allison, Morton's deputy at the National Committee, resigned and rejoined Treleaven in a new campaign management and consulting firm. Morton then hired Treleaven as a consultant to the Interior Department to study the entire public communications effort of the department and to recommend improvements.

While Treleaven was working as a consultant, his new firm, Allison, Treleaven and Reitz, submitted a proposal for a public communications program for the Bureau of Mines. The firm wanted a contract to design and run an advertising program that would urge miners to work more carefully. Treleaven's proposal would have kept the firm busy for the first few months of 1971 until the 1972 campaigns got into full swing. Word of the pending contract was leaked to the press and the Conservation Subcommittee of the House Operations Committee, and the contract did not go through. An attempt was then made to award the contract to a Nashville, Tenn., advertising firm with close connections to Allison, Treleaven and Reitz. That effort was stopped too, apparently by Interior Department staff lawyers who said no basis could be found for issuing a contract to a firm that had not even submitted a formal proposal.

While some managers find fun and profit combining campaign management and influence peddling, the bulk would rather campaign only. For those who do not try to pick what they have planted, the problems and conflicts of generating business year-round remain great.

The firms face a third major organizational reality. As they adapt and grow to meet organizational needs, they undergo quantitative and qualitive changes that often force them to abandon their original goals. This problem can be seen clearly in the contradiction between seeking work from party organizations to tide the firm through the off-season and the goal of being independent of the party hierarchy. One of the facts of organizational life is that goals change as the organization grows. The organizational realities, however, force those goals to change. The change is particularly painful to managers when they start accepting campaign clients they do not want to work for, either because they need the business or are afraid of alienating future business. Several managers complained about some of the candidates they "had" to work for because of obligations to statewide party committees. When one of the managers was asked how he described his work he responded that he was a "political mercenary." He said: "I became a political mercenary in 1966 after I worked for a couple of guys I didn't care for. My *present* goal requires that I be involved so I take whatever opportunity I have." Another firm, whose principals were avowedly anti-Nixon, accepted a contract to work on the Nixon campaign in one state because it could not afford to alienate either the state or national Republican committee.

One possible way to overcome the organizational need to grow and the consequent change in goals is to treat the campaign management firm as a temporary, task-oriented group rather than an organization. The firm can exist for the purpose of one election period and then collapse completely, only to be revived when the next campaign begins. Several theorists of organization, especially Warren Benis, have argued that this form of temporary organization is a wave of the future. The problem with this arrangement for the managers is that it does not even provide them with the myth of security. To admit from the outset that the firm has no basis for existing after the election is to admit to all the uncertainties the managers are trying to avoid.

While the industry and the professional managers have moved to the center of our electoral stage, their companies are still rather transient affairs. Both the problems and prospects for campaign management firms can be seen in microcosm in the experience of one firm, Bailey, Deardourff and Bowen. Its principals have made a determined effort to overcome all the organizational problems of institution building.

Bailey, Deardourff and Bowen, located in Washington, D.C., calls itself a "public issues communication" company. It does campaign planning, counseling and advertising for Republican candidates, and public issues advertising for corporate clients. The three principals in the firm have made a long-term commitment to building a professional and profitable campaign advertising company. Douglas Bailey was an assistant to Henry Kissinger at Harvard and also served as the staff director of the Wednesday Group, a collection of moderate and liberal Republican members of the House of Representatives. John Deardourff used to work for Nelson Rockefeller and was associate director of the domestic policy research staff for the 1964 Rockefeller campaign. In those days, Rockefeller and Lindsay were friendly so Deardourff directed the research effort for the Lindsay mayoral campaign in 1965. Both Bailey and Deardourff have long been committed to the idea that Rockefeller should be President of the United States. However, they tired of waiting around for the rest of the country to accept their idea. They are the firm's campaign planners and politicians. John Bowen is the advertising man. He came to Washington from Detroit where he was a vice president of Campbell-Ewald and media planner for the Chevrolet account, which is alleged to be the biggest advertising account in the world. Now, he would like everyone "to see the U.S.A." in a moderate Republican way. Stockholders in the firm include J. Irwin Miller, an industrialist and Republican activist who was *Esquire* magazine's "Perfect Presidential Candidate" in 1968, and Market Opinion Research, a Detroit polling company used by the firm.

The current company grew out of Campaign Consultants, Inc., which was founded by David Goldberg, a Boston attorney who planned the surprise Henry Cabot Lodge victory in the 1964 New Hampshire primary, and Bailey. The partners ran the firm on a part-time basis, accepting campaigns they thought would be interesting or important to the cause of liberal Republicanism. The Lodge victory in 1964 earned Goldberg a reputation within the Republican Party as something of a radical renegade. Nevertheless, the business grew in 1966. Clayton Gengras paid the firm a lot of money ($4,000 a month for the duration of his campaign) to help him in the gubernatorial election in Connecticut, which he lost. Most of the other clients that year lost, too, but they didn't pay as much to Campaign Consultants, Inc. In fact, six of C.C.I.'s seven clients in 1966 lost.

That record did not interfere with the firm's growth. There

was so much work that a third manager was added, Deardourff. In 1967, the partners worked on some winning campaigns, including the New Jersey state legislative races. Toward the end of the year, the firm signed a contract to run the Romney Presidential primary in New Hampshire in 1968. That ended when Romney was "brainwashed" out of the race and the partners returned to their favorite pursuit, the Presidency for Rockefeller. The horizontal expansion of the firm had proceeded well during its first three years. Starting from New England, the firm had received consulting contracts in states as far away as Ohio. In 1968, a vertical expansion also began. The firm acquired a company called Campaign Advertising, Inc., which was something of a paper organization that would allow it to keep some of the advertising commissions itself. The partners decided that advertising was where the money could be made in political consulting.

By 1968, Deardourff and Bailey felt that if the firm were to survive it would need full-time direction and would have to move to Washington, D.C. to be close to the political action. Goldberg was unwilling to leave Boston, so the original partnership dissolved and Goldberg continued to operate Campaign Consultants, Inc. much as he had in the past. In terms of the organizational realities discussed above, Campaign Consultants, Inc. could not adequately adapt to the demands of growth and the need to relate to the external environment.

In 1969, Deardourff and Bailey opened a new firm in Washington called Campaign Systems, Inc., offering essentially the same kind of management and counseling services the two had offered before. In the new company, however, the partners emphasized counseling instead of full management and were determined from the outset to get into advertising. A concentration on pre-campaign planning and counseling allowed them to achieve rapid expansion.

Both Campaign Consultants and Campaign Systems believed it to be useful to develop extensive relations with party leaders and candidates in a few states to develop a base. In a sense, the companies wanted to gain control over the party apparatus to insure future work—a classical organizational goal to make the environment safe for future operations. New Jersey was such a state. Deardourff worked closely with Nelson Gross, then Bergen County Republican leader, to plan and produce the Republican sweep of the state legislative elections in 1967. The firm continued to consult with Gross when he became state chairman and helped him reorganize the state committee. In 1968, the firm worked in New Jersey for the Nixon campaign. In 1969, it helped bring Gross and Cahill together and then ran Cahill's victorious primary and general election campaigns for governor. In 1970, the new firm of Bailey, Deardourff and Bowen consulted and did the campaign advertising for the Gross Senate campaign. Gross lost.

As the firm became more entrenched in New Jersey, the partners started establishing alternative bases in other states, especially in Pennsylvania, Ohio and Minnesota. Campaign Systems did consulting for a candidate in the Minneapolis mayoral election in 1969, almost entirely for the purpose of expanding its geographic base.

The experience of Bailey, Deardourff and Bowen in Pennsylvania shows some of the problems that can develop when a firm becomes entangled in state politics in addition to running campaigns. Campaign Consultants, Inc. did the preliminary campaign planning for the Schweiker for Senate contest in 1968 and during the campaign, the firm was employed as a regular consultant. One of the principals visited the state regularly to advise the campaign directors how to follow the plan written by the firm. Schweiker beat the incumbent, Joseph Clark, and credits the victory to the campaign and advertising strategy designed by the firm.

State Republican leaders were generally pleased with the job and accepted a proposal that the firm do a statewide management study for the party. This fit neatly into the company's plans to develop a strong base in the state. During the course of the study, members of the firm interviewed every major Republican leader in the state and examined every county operation. The contract helped carry the firm's expenses for the early part of 1969 and gave it an opportunity to line up contracts for the 1969 campaigns. As a result, the firm consulted in a statewide judgeship election and mayoral elections in Pittsburgh and Bethlehem. That was a bit more than it cared to do, but it was not in a position to say no because it was trying to keep people all over the state happy for the future.

While it may have been very helpful at the time, the firm's report on the state of the party in Pennsylvania laid the groundwork for future problems. Management reports by outside consultants almost always gore someone's sacred cow. This was no exception. Its general conclusion was that the party was in very weak shape, especially from a campaign manager's perspective. It reported, for example, that payoffs to the party were still being required before anyone got a public job in at least one county. That county chairman was more than a little unhappy with the report and its authors. The report suggested that all fund-raising be done on a centralized statewide basis. That may have made good management sense but it was a direct attack on the Philadelphia Republican organization, which had been very successful at doing its own fund-raising and had no intention of turning its access to resources over to the state. The Philadelphia Republican leader "blew a gasket" about the report and recommendations, in the words of one observer. As a result of its activities around the state, the firm began to collect some enemies.

The firm had a consulting and advertising contract for the 1970 gubernatorial campaign in Pennsylvania. When it arrived to tell the politicians how to run yet another campaign, there were some people "out to get them," and the conflict between the traditional party leaders and the modern consultants came out into the open. The formal campaign strategy and plans were ignored or undercut. Bailey, Deardourff and Bowen designed a plan to raise Raymond J. Broderick's favorable name recognition around the state. The traditional politicians wanted a campaign that went for the jugular vein of the opponent, a campaign that attacked Shapp. The full-time campaign director sent to the state from the Republican National Committee wanted a law and order campaign. At one point in the campaign, the Philadelphia Republican organization, through a front group called Citizens for a Better Pennsylvania, began running its own radio ads attacking Shapp. These ads upset the firm because they did not follow the campaign plan and because they were placed through another advertising agency. However, the hard-liners made their point and the firm started producing anti-Shapp material instead of the material it originally planned for the campaign.

Shapp won by a landslide with 55 percent of the total vote to Broderick's 42 percent. Some Broderick supporters took solace that they did not lose by more. Their private polls had shown Broderick 17 percentage points behind Shapp in October. The base Bailey, Deardourff and Bowen built so carefully was cracked badly, if not destroyed. The firm still had its strong supporters in the state, but its detractors now had a campaign full of stories and complaints. The firm was no longer the fair-haired savior of Pennsylvania Republicanism.

Even if Pennsylvania is no longer fertile ground, the firm has been working to build bases in other states. For example, it worked quite successfully in Delaware, Missouri and New York during the 1970 elections and its prospects for future work in those states are excellent. It is clear from the experience of Bailey, Deardourff and Bowen that firms must grow horizontally into new geographic areas if they are to protect themselves against complete disaster. It is also clear that working for state party organizations during the off-season has both real benefits and real hazards for future campaign work. The hazards are particularly severe if the firm loses a major campaign and if the people who are inevitably offended or threatened by change from the outside have a chance to get even. The members of the firm knew all this in theory; now they know it from experience.

Bailey, Deardourff and Bowen was set up as a successor to Campaign Systems to allow the firm to expand vertically into new areas of service, particularly advertising for both campaigns and corporations. Bailey and Deardourff had been frustrated in their roles as consultants, as well. All they had to sell was their time, which was limited by human factors, so the potential growth and impact of their operation was severely restricted. They wanted to create a company whose possible growth and involvement in campaigns was not limited to themselves alone. They felt they could create an expertise in political advertising that would break the company out of the bounds of personal consulting and make a lot of money. They could do the advertising for many campaigns through account executives and a creative team located in Washington. The principals of the firm might still do some consulting, but the heart of the business would not depend on that. They felt a new political advertising firm could compete successfully with regular commercial advertising agencies because of the recurring feeling against politics.

The new political advertising company was successful from a financial point of view. It handled very substantial advertising accounts for several major campaigns in 1970 and, for a new firm, made good money. The firm spent 1971 trying to establish commercial accounts. It made presentations to corporations stressing that, like it or not, they would have to deal with an environment of public opinion politics. The firm found some response to its pitch by mid-year.

While the advertising part of the business was growing slowly, the principals of the firm found that they had not yet achieved their goal of establishing a going business that did not depend on their personal consulting. In fact, they sold advertising to both campaigns and corporate clients because they could provide personal political consulting and planning. Instead of standing by itself, the advertising agency was dependent on the availability of the principals of the firm for political consulting.

In 1969, Bailey said that people came to Campaign Systems because they wanted Deardourff or him. Most of the customers could never quite remember the name of the firm. The same appeared to be true of the new company. Its appeal was still the personal services of the principal members of the firm. There seemed to be no incentive for people to hire it just as an advertising agency. Bailey, Deardourff and Bowen remained optimistic that their original plans for a self-sustaining political advertising firm would develop. In the meantime, they were doing a lot of personal consulting in order to sell advertising.

That they were having a difficult though profitable time is an indication of the problems faced by the firms that pay little attention to their organizational needs. In the process of moving from a part-time firm in Boston with no overhead to a full-time organization in Washington with heavy overhead expenses, the goals of the original partners went through subtle but important changes. When they were in Boston, the partners talked about strengthening the liberal wing of the Republican Party. It was their stated goal to work in campaigns that would strengthen their wing of the party or make some important ideological point, such as their conviction Republicans could win in urban areas by taking progressive positions. Later, the organizational demands of the firm were their first concern. They were still interested in promoting moderate and liberal Republicans but that was no longer the stated goal. It was more a long-term hope.

Bailey, Deardourff and Bowen was established with the explicit goal of becoming the dominant political advertising firm in the country with annual billings in excess of ten million dollars by 1973. The partners were strongly anti-Nixon in 1968, but they wound up working for him to preserve their position in New Jersey. The principals of the firm have some people they would like to work for who are "their kind" of Republicans. They keep wanting to go out and solicit their business because they think the firm can help. That was the plan in both 1969 and 1971: decide who it is important to help and go after his business. However, that has not really happened. There was not enough time or flexibility to do that kind of planning and gambling. Rather, the firm wound up taking the candidates who came to it and the candidates in the states it had already worked so hard to develop. The results were financially fruitful for the firm, but frustrating to the original goals of its founders.

The example of Bailey, Deardourff and Bowen—its mix of goals and motivations, its change because of the practicalities of continued existence, its loss of idealism—indicates the hard realities that face all the professional campaign managers. Whether or not they survive in their present form is an open question, but they will survive in one way or another. In their operations, they profoundly influence the parties and the candidates for whom they work and, more important, the political process of American democracy and the American people.

CHAPTER 9

The Threat
to Democracy

> To be venturesome, young, rich and have some favor-
> able public identification is to be the perfect political
> candidate for the managers of image politics.

> Elections will be based on pseudo-events communi-
> cated by television or temporary outpourings of vol-
> unteers.

The professional campaign managers are a small group of
businessmen-politicians who are taking control of the electoral process in the United States. They are using their skills
in modern research and communications to make decisions
that change both the process and content of American politics. What they do affects all of us.

The political process, especially elections, gives the people
some opportunity to keep their leaders in check. But today
many of the crucial decisions of elections—who shall run and
what they shall say—are decided not by the people or even
by their organized leaders, but by small groups of professional
managers and money men. Who is to check the professional
campaign managers?

The presence of public accountability for their actions is
a traditional test that has been relied upon heavily by supporters of the theories of democratic elitism and pluralism
to reconcile the existence of elites with democracy; small
groups may hold power as long as they remain accountable
to the masses. In its simplest form, accountability means going
back to the people or groups to whom you have done or
promised something for a judgment about your performance.
In the American political system, political accountability has

always depended in substantial part on the existence of fixed geographic political boundaries. Thus, political leaders always had to return to the same place for a reckoning. The flexibility of professional managers which allows them to intervene at different levels and widely varying geographic locations makes it virtually impossible to fix responsibility for their actions. Similarly, the temporary organizations the managers create to win an election do not remain after the election to hold either the firm or the candidate responsible for what was done and said in the campaign. Even corporate executives can sometimes be held responsible for their decisions by their boards of directors, employees and customers because they take place within an identifiable institutional structure. However, when a political campaign is over, the professional manager and the organization he created are gone.

In individual campaigns, the professional managers may be accountable for their actions to the candidate and his committee. However, where the management firm has the responsibility for recruiting the candidate and teaching him what he needs to know about politics, it is difficult to rely on this route of accountability.

Since most of the professional managers work for candidates in only one political party, it might be said that they are held accountable to the national leaders and candidates of that party. On examination, this is not really a satisfactory system of accountability. First, many party structures themselves suffer from an insulation from real public accountability. How does the public get at the Congressional Campaign Committees of both parties? They raise and spend millions of dollars of special interest money without being responsible to anybody but a small group of well-entrenched members of Congress. An industry that has grown because the parties are weak cannot be said to be checked by them. Further, the geographic mobility of the managers affects the ability of local and state parties to hold them accountable. In many cases, the managers are hired by a party committee at the national level to work on a campaign at the local level. Even if the firm is accountable to the national party committee, it is free from effective control of the group with which it is actually working at the local level.

In still other cases, the professional management firms may be responsible to the interest groups that hired them. But to whom are the interest groups themselves responsible? One of the central criticisms of pluralist democracy is that the major groups are internally undemocratic and irresponsible. If the members of these special interest groups cannot influence what they do, how are the rest of us to hold them accountable for the millions of dollars they invest in politics?

The only accountability that seems to operate is the win-lose record of a firm. If a particular firm loses too often, it probably will go out of business. But if a firm wins its share of elections there is no way to hold it accountable either for the specific things it does in campaigns or for the impact of its techniques on the political system as a whole.

Thus, a new political elite is developing at the very core of democracy that does not meet a crucial test, a relationship of responsibility to the people. The professional managers and their techniques of controlled mass communication have the tools to undo all the steps we have taken toward mass democracy. The campaign managers are increasingly accountable only to themselves and to their own vision of politics. And, under contract, they give others the ability to intervene in politics without needing to account for their presence or actions either.

In fact, the unresponsibility of professional campaign management is one of its principal attractions both to the managers themselves and to the people who use their services. The managers can be active in politics without actually having to accept any public responsibilities. They can be independent and have professional respect, and the people who pay for politics can get what they need without investing in permanent organizations or without being publicly identified either with their actions or the outcome. For the elites, it is a perfect set-up.

Further, the professional managers are weakening democracy by their perceptions of what politics ought to be and through the techniques they are introducing to American politics. They share in the blame for weakening our democracy because they have a narrow view of what politics is all about, because they help build temporary rather than real political organizations, because they introduce techniques that minimize and discourage political participation rather than maximize it, and because they have failed to account for the social impact of their technological innovations in politics.

Of course no matter what they think or do, professional campaign managers will not alone destroy or deliver democracy. There are many other factors involved. However, the professional managers are far more than neutral merchandisers of political techniques. They themselves are not neutral, and what they do in politics affects the system as a whole.

Professional campaign managers are not neutral because their technocratic approach to politics brings a "scientific ideology" into electoral politics. The technocratic approach to politics, based on formally researched information and direct mass communication, is different from traditional politics. A democratic election is both a contest over who shall rule and a test of the system itself. In this traditional idea, an election is a situation of conflict and choice. That is not so for the technocratic politics of the campaign managers. For them, an election is a problem to be solved, just as aircraft noise is a problem for an engineer to solve. Neither needs to deal with the questions of conflict and choice that are related to their "problems."

Both traditional and modern campaigners need to win election contests. However, the problem-solving orientation of professional managers causes them to approach elections differently than traditional politicians. For the traditional political leader, the election is just one element of a continuing political organizing task and only one function of the political party. For the professional campaign manager, the election is the only problem. He does not have to be concerned with anything else. Thus, the professional manager is free to apply the tools of formal research and mass communication to achieve a solution to his campaign problem without relating to any other aspects of politics. The options available to a traditional politician are much more limited by his past commitments.

Bruce Merrill, a professional pollster and consultant, has said that as an analyst he welcomes the idea that the opponent have the same high quality research he uses because then the election will be a real contest of skill, the skill of finding among the data an electoral majority for his candidate and showing his candidate how to reap the benefit of it. His campaign polling and consulting firm's introductory brochure begins:

> The computer in politics—a new approach to the elective process . . . After revolutionizing business and science, the computer has entered the political arena . . . To the campaign manager, elected officeholder and party policy makers, this means that for the first time he is offered a comprehensive modular approach to campaigning.

But what difference does all of this make? In the environment of technology, different people and different organizational forms will dominate electoral politics and most of us will not have very much to say about it.

Two of the characteristics of professional campaign management combine to help a new kind of candidate emerge in American politics. First, the professional managers, as agents of change and modernization, need to find innovators to adopt their ideas. Second, the professionals, as organizers who are solving the problems of the campaign, know that one type of candidate is obviously better suited to solving a particular campaign problem than another. They help find these innovator-candidates.

The definition of the kind of person who is an innovator sounds very much like the kind of person who has been emerging in electoral politics in recent years in the hands of the professional campaign managers. The innovator is venturesome, young, has high social status, is wealthy, has close contact with scientific information, makes great use of impersonal sources of information, interacts with other innovators, has some experience as an opinion leader and has a cosmopolitan outlook.

In this way, the professional managers are helping to change the qualifications for running for office in the United States. The traditional qualities of party regularity, a geographic political base of some kind and an ability to assess the mood of the people are being replaced. Now, to be venturesome, young, rich and have some favorable public identification is to be the perfect political candidate for the managers of image politics.

As Stanley Kelley has said, the traditional characteristics of desirability and availability have changed:

> The public relations man tends to gauge availability [for public office] by measures of the currency a candidate's name enjoys with the public, the success with which he has projected a public personality and the attitudes excited by his personality.

When this kind of candidate does not appear by himself to run in a particular election, professional campaign managers have sometimes been hired to find him. They look for people who have orientations like their own, who will rely on research information, be able to use mass media and who have or are able to raise the money needed to pay for a modern campaign.

As the cycle of change moves beyond innovation to general acceptance of these new professional techniques, they may be used by more traditional political personalities to keep themselves in office. That is what happened among incumbent United States Senators in 1970. Almost all the Democratic incumbents used the services of campaign managers to stave off the professionally-managed Republican attack. They used the new techniques, too.

The information-based system of the professional campaign managers is bringing to the fore again the traditional debate about the meaning of representation in democratic government. Several of the professional managers argue that their techniques make true democratic representation possible for the first time because through constant polling they can continuously inform public officials how the public feels about an issue.

In the view of some of the managers, the public official need never be troubled about not knowing what to do on a controversial issue. He can take a poll and vote the way his constituents feel on an issue. This may be a simplistic view of representation, but it is proposed by some of the managers as the first advance on the subject since Edmund Burke spoke to his electors at Bristol.

The prospect for this debate in American representative theory was raised by a delegate to a political party research seminar in 1969. The delegate asked the professional campaign manager and pollster who was giving the seminar whether the local political committee should take a survey to find out what the people want and then recruit a candidate who meets those criteria or whether it should take the survey after it chooses the candidate and have him adapt his own views to conform to the findings. Both alternatives completely ignored the idea that leaders should lead.

As the professional managers' ideas about the election process and the importance of formal research in winning elections become dominant, they are changing the shape of and the participants in political party organizations. Nimmo found these changes to be taking place in the political party organizations he observed. He reported:

> In advising on the restructuring of state and local parties, the campaign technicians reorganize to fit parties to the management conception of what an election is all about. The party assumes a new "image" but not one necessarily appropriate for its traditional supporters who find themselves replaced by new recruits.

One manager interviewed for this study indicated with pleasure that his firm, Politicon, had completely reorganized a county committee's operations and brought many new people in to take over party positions. Politicon's introductory brochure says the new politics is the application of the principles of modern systems management to achieve the marketing objective of the political executive management. It continues:

> In any successful business today, management relies heavily on the quantity and quality of information gleaned from market research and analyses. Political marketing has much the same basic need. The first step of the successful political organization and/or candidate for office is to create a reservoir of pertinent marketing information.

The goal of organizing information about people to win elections is substantially different from the goal of organizing people to win elections. The professional managers would use the parties to organize information. For them, a party is a strong central staff with up-to-date information about the people who live in its area. The resource base of the party, then, is the information management system. With this resource, the central committee can raise funds, recruit candidates and fashion an electoral majority for them.

Creating parties without people does not necessarily mean that managers do not think people can be an important campaign tool. Some managers create large temporary organizations to mobilize the candidate's potential majority. These temporary organizations are sometimes capable of producing thousands of workers in a campaign. However, when the campaign is over, neither the manager nor any political organization remains.

A party without people is even more convenient for the strategies that emphasize formal mass media communication. Large numbers of people in the party or campaign who need to be dealt with are just nuisances who get in the way of communicating directly with the even larger number of voters who are not active. Television, direct mail and computer-operated phone banks make this possible, and professional managers who can use these tools provide leaders with a relatively inexpensive alternative to genuine political organization.

The management conception of a political party may well usher in a new stage of American party development. The popular bases of the party would continue to diminish. Small national and state staffs would commission formal research and buy direct advertising communication to mobilize the portion of the population that chooses to participate in elections. The distinction between a party and an interest group would be virtually lost. The rewards of winning would be relevant only to the people running the "party" and paying the bills.

There will be no real participation in the party system run by professional managers. Rather elections will be based on the pseudo-events communicated by television or temporary outpourings of volunteers. Effective control and direction will remain with the few at the top. Governments would be selected through elections but the continuing legitimacy of the system would need to be tested in other ways. Professionally-managed politics will not address the individual's need for self-development. In fact, the individual's needs will be irrelevant.

In a recent article, Walter Dean Burnham concluded:

> American electoral politics is undergoing a long-term transition into routines designed only to fill offices and symbolically affirm the "American way." There also seem to be tendencies for our political parties gradually to evaporate as broad and active intermediaries between the people and their rulers, even as they may well continue to maintain enough organizational strength to screen out the unacceptable or the radical at the nominating stage.

If this pattern develops, it shall have been made possible in part by the professional campaign management firms that taught parties and candidates how to run and win elections without people.

Political power in the new party system will go to those who have or buy information about the electorate and the know-how to mobilize voters without involving them. In the strong urban political parties of the past, the "boss" and his precinct leaders kept control because they had a virtual monopoly on political intelligence and mobilizing capability. In the new party system, such a monopoly will be harder to maintain because the formalized research techniques of science are replicable and because the mass media are available to whoever can pay for it. However, while anyone could do the research and plan the media, it is the professional campaign managers who will have the cumulative experience and skills to do the research and use the media most effectively.

The other principal resource of power in the new party system will be money. Money has always been important in American politics. In the technocratic party system, money will be even more important because it is the most flexible resource. Money can be used to purchase other resources, like information and skilled managers. In previous party systems, other resources like manpower and patronage were often more important than money as campaign tools.

Thus the new party system will again provide stability and

order to the people who pay for politics. Professional management firms already serve this function at the local and state level in a few parts of the country. In California, Whitaker and Baxter brought order to politics for the oil companies, the public utilities, the railroads and the large farmers for more than 20 years. Baus and Ross did the same for the real estate, banking, home construction and oil interests in Los Angeles. Decision Making Information is now attempting to do the same thing for the American Medical Association Political Action Committee, which has become the largest single contributor to Republican Congressional candidates.

The professionally-managed political system will continue the trend toward a nationalization of politics. It allows an interested and well-financed group to intervene at almost any level of the party system. That is beginning to happen now. The research and campaign counseling activities of the national party campaign organizations described in earlier chapters are an attempt by the national committees of the parties to organize, finance and conduct essentially local contests for national offices from the national level. State parties, especially in California, are doing the same thing when they intervene in local state legislative races. These represent big steps in the attempt to build electoral victories from the top down using the shell of parties.

Even though few of the firms have survived over long periods, the managers believe that they themselves can become the non-temporary element in electoral politics. This tremendous potential for power is not lost on some of the professional management firms. Several of the Republican firms cooperate in formal and informal ways waiting on the day that they shall be able to take over the Republican Party and "elect a President who is worth electing." They are doing several things to make that day come sooner. These firms maintain ownership of the information they gather on research contracts and one of them now owns an extensive data bank on voters in several states. They have made deliberate attempts to develop continuing contractual relationships with party organizations in different parts of the country to insert their view of politics in party re-organization and they have agreed to work for candidates they do not really like to gather the information base they will need to take over the party. Whether they will succeed remains to be seen. In the process of trying, however, they may well reshape major elements of the party into their own image of what politics ought to be.

In the 20th century we have turned to political elites to run our government and politics to protect democracy from the instability of the masses. The emergence of a new elite of managers at the center of electoral politics may be the culmination of this process and we may soon realize that democracy has been weakened again by our latest attempt to protect it. Perhaps that has been happening all along from our reliance on elites. To protect democracy, they have prevented it, and, to keep our society stable, they have made it rigid. Mass political parties were the best weapon ever invented to check the power of elites. Now, as a new commercial-political elite begins to control the very institutions that were developed to check elites, it may become clearer to all of us that democracy is best protected by the active engagement and social development of its citizens. It may be possible to get political power through a 60-second spot but democracy will take more than that.

Chapter Notes

Chapter 1   *The New Gang In Town*

In 1972 the Muskie, Humphrey, Lindsay, Mills and Nixon campaigns were almost wholly designed and run by professional campaign managers and professional campaign management firms. The McGovern campaign was a mixture of ideologically oriented professionals and volunteers and professional media men. McGovern's ability to use both traditional grass roots organizing and professional media campaigning was a key to his early success.

The pundits' books referred to include: Kevin P. Phillips, *The Emerging Republican Majority* (New Rochelle: Arlington House, 1969); Richard M. Scammon and Ben J. Wattenberg, *The Real Majority* (New York: Coward, 1970); Frederick P. Dutton, *Changing Sources of Power* (New York: McGraw Hill, 1971); and Walter DeVries and V. Lance Tarrence, *The Ticket Splitter* (Grand Rapids: Eerdmans, 1972).

Estimating campaign expenditures is a tricky business. Until April 1972, the reporting laws that governed campaigns were a complete farce. The laws have been rewritten, but so much money was raised early in the year before the new regulations went into effect that it will be several years before we know whether or not the new laws are effective at disclosing the amounts and sources of political money. My own estimate of current spending, which is somewhat higher than other campaign watchers', grows from research I did on campaign spending sponsored by the Twentieth Century Fund in 1970. See *Electing Congress, The Financial Dilemma* (New York: Twentieth Century Fund, 1970).

The Federal Communications Commission requires radio and television stations to file accurate reports on free and commercial time made available for political campaigning. These reports are summarized and printed after each Presidential and Congressional election by the Federal Communications Commission.

The growth in television spending between 1968 and 1970 is even more dramatic than the figures indicate because the 1960

169

and 1968 figures include the 15 percent advertising agency fee while the 1970 report excludes them. Using the 1968 calculating method, 1970 spending was about 57 million dollars.

Accurate figures on the skyrocketing costs of producing television and radio political commercials are available only through interviews with candidates and professional managers. In early 1972 many professionals were predicting that the new limits on the amount of money a candidate could spend on commercial time on radio and television would send production costs up even further because each candidate would want to be sure that the best possible product was being used in the limited time he had available on radio and television.

The Political Marketplace (New York: Quadrangle, 1972), which I edited, was the first attempt to collect information about all the professional managers and to make it available to the general public in directory form. Among other things, the directory lists the companies and indexes more than 40 different services offered by professional campaign managers and suppliers.

There are countless books about democracy and about elections. The ones I found most helpful in writing this chapter and which I would recommend to anyone wishing to explore these ideas further are Peter Bachrach, *The Theory of Democratic Elitism* (Boston: Little Brown, 1967); Walter Dean Burnham, *Critical Elections and the Mainsprings of American Politics* (New York: W. W. Norton, 1970); Gerald Pomper, *Elections in America* (New York: Dodd, Mead, 1970); V. O. Key, *The Responsible Electorate* (New York: Vintage, 1968); Stanley Kelley, *Public Relations and Political Power* (Baltimore: Johns Hopkins Press, 1956); Dan Nimmo, *The Political Persuaders* (Englewood Cliffs: Prentice Hall, 1970); and James Perry, *The New Politics* (New York: Clarkson Potter, 1968).

Chapter 2   *The Emergence of the Professionals*

The opening quotes are typical of the campaign slogans that dominated the 1970 and 1972 elections. Thomas Kleppe's remarks are quoted from a story by Nick Kotz in the Washington *Post*, November 22, 1971. During the 1970 campaigns papers like the

Washington *Post,* the Washington *Evening Star* and the New York *Times* made a special effort to cover the advertising and professional management aspects of the campaigns as well as the activities of the candidates themselves. Much of the detail included in this chapter grows from leads provided in stories by good political reporters like Robert Walters of the Washington *Evening Star,* Nick Kotz of the Washington *Post* and R. W. Apple of the New York *Times.*

The quotation from Stanley Kelley is drawn from *Public Relations and Political Power.* Kelley was one of the first and the best academic observers of the trend toward commercial campaigning.

The figures on the growth of the professional campaign management industry at different levels of the political system grow from the research done for this book. I asked professional campaign managers to outline all the services they provided to campaigns since 1960. I received reliable data from more than 150 firms. This was combined with information published early in the decade in Alexander Heard, *The Costs of Democracy* (Chapel Hill: University of North Carolina Press, 1960). A much more detailed description of the growth of the industry is available in my unpublished Ph.D. thesis, *Managers in Politics,* Massachusetts Institute of Technology, Cambridge, 1970.

The letter from the Utah Republican leaders to the White House was reported in the New York *Times,* March 7, 1971. It reflected similar criticisms voiced by party leaders in many other states.

F. Clifton White's story of the 1970 Buckley for Senate campaign was most fully told at a seminar on the 1970 elections sponsored by the American Association of Political Consultants. The association has held seminars after each recent election to allow the managers an opportunity to gloat, complain and compare notes.

Joseph Napolitan has now published his own version of the 1966 Shapp election campaign in his book, *The Election Game and How to Win it* (New York: Doubleday, 1972).

Shortly after the 1966 election Spencer-Roberts published its own mimeographed description of the role it played in the campaign. The information included in this chapter about the Reagan gubernatorial and Presidential campaigns comes from interviews conducted in 1969, 1970 and 1971 with Stu Spencer and Bill Roberts (in 1969) and many other professional politicians, party leaders, government officials and political observers in California.

Chapter 3 *The Tools of the Trade*

Vincent Barabba and Matt Reese, whose remarks open this chapter, are among the best professional managers in the country. They were very cooperative throughout this project, submitting to several long interviews and letting me go through some of their materials.

Napolitan includes a description of his role in the 1968 Humphrey campaign in his book referred to above. Jack Chestnut, Humphrey's 1970 manager, provided a complete description of that campaign at an American Association of Political Consultants meeting in New York in November, 1970.

The quote from George Washington Plunkitt is drawn from a delightful book by William Riordan, *Plunkitt of Tammany Hall* (New York: Dutton, 1963).

Spencer-Roberts includes the good piece of advice from Lincoln on the cover of all the reports they send to candidates. They argue that computers and telephone banks and all the other paraphernalia of modern campaigning just make the traditional goal possible.

The material on the different forms of polling now being used in campaigns comes from interviews and mail questionnaires completed by virtually all of the major political pollsters in the country.

Walter DeVries presents most of his research about ticket-splitters in the book by that name referred to above. He has used his research techniques with very good results, especially in Michigan where he has been heavily involved in the campaigns of George Romney and William G. Milliken.

The Schweicker for Senate campaign plan was made available to me by people connected with the campaign. It does not differ in many details from campaign plans prepared by other professional managers in both parties. I interviewed both Douglas Bailey and John Deardourff several times and they were very helpful.

Chapter 4 *How It All Began*

The material on Whitaker and Baxter was gathered from previously written descriptions of the firm and from interviews with political observers in California. The principal written reference works were: chapters two and three of Stanley Kelley's *Political Public Relations*, cited above; Carey McWilliams, "Government by Whitaker and Baxter, The Triumph of Gold-Plated Publicity," *The Nation*, April 14, 21 and May 5, 1951; Everett Kindig, "The Professional Campaign: A Study of Political Public Relations in California Politics," unpublished master's thesis at Stanford University, 1962; and occasional speeches and articles written by Whitaker and Baxter themselves and available in the files of Whitaker and Baxter, International.

The quote from Miss Baxter about the firm's role in the 1934 campaign against Upton Sinclair is drawn from an article on the firm by Stephan McNamara that appeared in the San Francisco *Examiner*'s *People Magazine*, September 3, 1965. In the 1934 campaign Whitaker and Baxter formally worked for the Republican candidate for lieutenant governor and against Sinclair. They did not run the campaign for the Republican candidate for governor, Frank Merriam, though their attacks on Sinclair helped him win.

Only a small portion of Alexander Heard's monumental study of money in politics was concerned with political public relations. The material cited in this chapter may be found in Alexander Heard, *The Costs of Democracy*, cited above, p. 417.

Maurice Duverger, *Political Parties* (London: Methuen, 1954), argues the connection between legal structure and the patterns of party development throughout the book.

Hiram Johnson was a progressive governor of California early in the 20th century. Some of the laws he had written to destroy political parties and allow for popular referenda are still on the books. Others have been repealed. For example, the law which allowed candidates to file in the primary of both parties was finally repealed in 1963. But while it was in force, Earl Warren won both the Republican and Democratic primaries for two of his terms as governor of California.

Samuel Hays' article "Political Parties and the Community-

Society Continuum" appears in William Chambers and Walter Burnham, *The American Party Systems, Stages of Development* (New York: Oxford, 1967). This reader is an excellent collection of articles on the past and future of American political parties.

Figures on voting participation are drawn from Congressional Quarterly, *Congress and the Nation, Vol. II* (Washington: Congressional Quarterly, 1969). Figures on population growth and urbanization come from U.S. Bureau of the Census, *Statistical Abstract of the United States, 1968* (Washington: U.S. Government Printing Office, 1968). The information on AMPAC contributions comes, in part, from a New York *Times* story on December 9, 1969.

There is a growing literature on the effects of television on politics and society. Among the sources used for the conclusions drawn in this chapter are: Tony Schwartz, "The Global Village," *Communications Arts*, 1969; Joseph Klapper, *The Effects of Mass Communication* (New York: Free Press, 1960); Harry Skornia, *Television and Society* (New York: McGraw-Hill, 1965); Kurt and Gladys Lang, *Politics and Television* (Chicago: Quadrangle, 1968); Marshall McLuhan, *Understanding Media* (New York: McGraw-Hill, 1964); Nicholas Johnson, *How to Talk Back to Your Television Set* (Boston: Little Brown, 1970); Jay Blumler and Denis McQuail, *Television in Politics* (Chicago: University of Chicago Press, 1969), an excellent study of the effects of television on British campaigns; and Angus Campbell, "Has Television Reshaped Politics?" *Columbia Journalism Review*, I (1962), pp. 10–13.

The cited article by Harold Lasswell is "The Propagandist Bids for Power," *American Scholar*, 8 (1939). Louise Overacker's *Money in Politics* (New York: Macmillan, 1932) is an excellent discussion of the connection between business and the Republicans early in the century. Robert Merton's *Social Theory and Social Functions, Revised* (New York: Free Press, 1957) discusses the connection between business and old-line party machines. More recent works on business in politics that were used for this chapter include: John K. Galbraith, *The New Industrial State* (Boston: Houghton-Mifflin, 1967); Andrew Hacker, "Businessmen in Politics," *Law and Contemporary Problems*, 27

(1962); and Edwin Epstein, *The Corporation in American Politics* (Englewood Cliffs: Prentice Hall, 1969).

Chapter 5 *Where Did They Come From?*

The opening quotes are drawn from an article by Joe McGinness on Matt Reese that appeared in the Philadelphia *Inquirer* in 1967, from a *Newsweek* cover story on professional campaign managers, October 19, 1970, and from a personal interview. The great bulk of the information in this chapter comes from interviews with professional campaign managers around the country. However, a few articles and books proved helpful. Joe McGinniss' description of the 1968 Nixon campaign, *The Selling of the President, 1968* (New York: Trident, 1969), was very helpful. The *National Journal* consistently does the best job keeping track of the professional managers and I relied heavily on the article on the 1970 campaign published in the October 3, 1970 issue.

Richard Harris, "How's It Look?" *New Yorker*, April 8, 1967, is an excellent description of Otis Pike's traditional campaign style.

Managers are beginning to write about themselves. Two such books used for this chapter are: Herbert Baus and William Ross, *Politics: Battle Plan* (New York: Macmillan, 1968) and Joseph Napolitan, *The Election Game and How to Win It*, cited above.

Chapter 6 *Amateurs and Professionals*

Joe Napolitan's sexual analogy, taken from his book, was similar to statements made by many other managers. Most of the others were more graphic. One interviewee who had retired from the business said that "most professionals would rather campaign than screw. I have a different set of priorities, so I got out." The remaining opening quotes came from interviews.

The amateur-professional dichotomy has been most thoroughly explored by James Wilson, *The Amateur Democrat* (Chicago: University of Chicago Press, Phoenix Books, 1966).

Dan Nimmo's *The Political Persuaders* has been cited already. The material used in this chapter appears on p. 65. Ernest Greenwood, "Attributes of a Profession," *Social Work*, 2, No. 3 (July, 1957), pp. 44–55 and Corine Lathrop Gills, *Hidden Hierarchies: The Professions in Government* (New York: Harper and Row, 1966), chapter one, were used as guides to the formal definition of a profession.

Chapter 7 *The Managers and the Political Parties*

We owe a good deal of what we know about the American electorate to the Michigan University Survey Research Center. Its staff has been conducting regular studies of the attitudes and behavior of the electorate for more than 20 years. Angus Campbell, *et al.*, *The American Voter* (New York: Wiley, 1960); and Philip Converse, *et al.*, "Continuity and Change in American Politics: Parties and Issues in the 1968 Election," *American Political Science Review*, 63, no. 4 (December, 1969), pp. 1083–1106, were particularly helpful for this chapter. Another post-1968 election article that has been important for the conclusions reached here is Walter Burnham, "The End of American Party Politics," *Transaction*, December, 1969.

Most of the quotations from campaign managers come from personal interviews. However, the remarks attributed to Harry Treleaven were reported in *Newsweek*, October 19, 1970, p. 36, and the quotation from Bill Roberts appeared in a Republican National Committee publication entitled *The Art of Winning Elections* (Washington: Republican National Committee, undated).

Chapter 8 *Will They Survive?*

Much of the theoretical framework for this chapter is drawn from Daniel Katz and Robert Kahn, *The Social Psychology of Organizations* (New York: Wiley, 1966).

The material on Spencer-Roberts and Bailey, Deardourff and Bowen comes from interviews with the principals and other politicians with whom they have worked. The Bailey, Deardourff and Bowen material was supplemented by reference to Peter A. Herndorf and C. Edward Ward, "The Business of Politics: The Economics of the Political Consulting Industry" an unpublished master's thesis, Harvard Business School, 1970. The authors made virtually all the fruits of their research available to me.

Warren Benis is one of our most creative thinkers and writers on organizational problems. The article referred to in this chapter is "Beyond Bureaucracy," *Transaction*, July-August, 1965.

Chapter 9   *The Threat to Democracy*

The notion of accountability for political elites is discussed extensively in a great deal of the modern literature in political theory. An outstanding summary of the debate is included in the book by Peter Bachrach cited above.

The import of a technocratic approach to politics should not be underestimated. The essence of politics is choice, among possible leaders, parties and policies. Technocratic politics is an attempt to transcend the problems of choice and uncertainty. The technocratic approach is more than a technique, as Sanford Lakoff has suggested. It is a desire for objective standards and guidance and thus it becomes an ideology itself.

Bruce Merrill's remarks were made at a seminar of the Atlantic Association of Young Political Leaders in Washington, D.C., May 9, 1969. His firm, Bruce Merrill Associates, is a subsidiary of University Computing Company in Dallas. The brochure quoted is entitled "Consider the Computer in Politics."

A very complete review of the literature about the kinds of people who are innovators is found in Everett Rogers, *Diffusion of Innovation* (New York: Free Press, 1962).

The quotation from Kelley may be found in *Public Relations and Political Power*, cited above, page 219. The quotation from Nimmo may be found in *The Political Persuaders*, cited above, page 67. Politicon's brochure is entitled "A New Concept in Political Marketing."

The quotation from Walter Dean Burnham is taken from his article "The End of American Party Politics," cited above, page 20.

Index